BUILDING PROJECTS IN CHINA

A MANUAL FOR ARCHITECTS AND ENGINEERS

BERT BIELEFELD

LARS-PHILLIP RUSCH

BUILDING PROJECTS IN CHINA
A MANUAL FOR ARCHITECTS AND ENGINEERS

BIRKHÄUSER – PUBLISHERS FOR ARCHITECTURE
BASEL · BOSTON · BERLIN

Illustrations: page 41, 121, 198 by Bert Bielefeld, all other illustrations by the respective authors

Translation into English: Michael Robinson, London
English copy editing: Lucy Byatt, Edinburgh

This book is also available in a German language edition (ISBN 3-7643-7415-2).

A CIP catalogue record for this book is available from the
Library of Congress, Washington D.C., USA

Bibliographic information published by Die Deutsche Bibliothek.
Die Deutsche Bibliothek lists this publication in the Deutsche
Nationalbibliographie; detailed bibliographic data is available in the
internet at <http://dnb.ddb.de>.

© 2006 Birkhäuser – Publishers for Architecture,
P.O. Box 133, CH-4010 Basel, Switzerland
Part of Springer Science + Business Media

Printed on acid-free paper produced from chlorine-free pulp. TCF ∞
Printed in Germany

ISBN-10: 3-7643-7416-0
ISBN-13: 978-3-7643-7416-7

9 8 7 6 5 4 3 2 1
www.birkhauser.ch

Contents

Foreword

Many architecture practices proudly show off gigantic projects they have realized in the Middle Kingdom. Any self-respecting architect tries his luck in China – or so it would seem. High growth rates make it possible for companies and private individuals to bring off audacious projects speedily. This is particularly true of building. Building projects in booming Chinese regions are impressive in their number and scale, as can currently be seen from the business sections and feature pages of European daily papers.

There are well-trained architects and town planners all over the world and competition is fierce internationally. Training standards are continuously rising in China itself, but the qualities of German and European architecture and town planning and European architects', engineers' and town planners' skills are particularly sought after in China. This benefits German architects, engineers and town planners in international competitions. Their innovative abilities, particularly in the technical sphere, are another important factor.

Stepping over the border into China opens up a lot of opportunities: exploiting new market potential, realizing extraordinary projects, and getting to know a different culture. Planning and building in China offer foreign planners extensive possibilities for putting their visions into practice and developing their skills.

But a step abroad should always be taken cautiously. Non-Asiatic planning practices have some hoops to jump through in China: considerably more effort has to be made to gain commissions there; cultural differences can trigger misunderstandings and many projects can be difficult to carry out because of the geographical distances involved and the need to be frequently present on the spot. So it is important to be well informed about opportunities and risks in China. Anyone who is seriously interested in a planning job in China should be on a stable financial footing at home and have intercultural skills and an affinity with Chinese people and culture.

In Germany the Federal Chamber of Architects, the umbrella organization of the German Chambers of Architects, supports this step abroad through the NAX architecture export network. NAX aims to promote the exchange of information and experience between German and foreign planners, entrepreneurs and developers and to use targeted marketing to establish links and thus to increase architects' opportunities in foreign markets, including China. This will make it easier to exchange architects' services across borders and increase their professional mobility worldwide. For this reason, we welcome *Building Projects in China* as a sound and important contribution providing serious information and assistance, and also promoting architectural interest in a country as unique as China.

This volume in the *Building Projects* series offers an introduction to the complex market conditions in China and provides a platform for experienced freelancers from Germany and other Western countries. Chapter A introduces readers to Chinese town planning and the development of architecture from traditional housing to the present day. Chapter B explains the basic commercial and legal conditions for successful planning work in China. In Chapter C, planners actually working in China advise on market entry and attracting business, possibilities for setting up branches, the commercial viability of commissions, the way Chinese planning practices work, and also how to behave in China. Chapter D features classic reports of experiences in China, with presentations of individual projects. The appendix rounds off the volume with important addresses and a bibliography.

Dr Thomas Welter, commercial and business adviser, Netzwerk Architekturexport (NAX)

China as a booming market

A 1 China's economic development

Dr Bert Bielefeld / Lars-Phillip Rusch

Foreign architects and engineers cannot equate the demands made by planning, building and working with Chinese planners and clients with their experiences in America and Europe. China is the liveliest market worldwide and has an individual character developed from a mixture of traditional, socialist and market-economy influences.

The economy and development

A glance at the economic data for the People's Republic of China can be a source of astonishment. The country has become the sixth largest economy and the third largest trading nation in the space of just ten years, and yet China is also the largest developing country on earth, with an average income per head of just over 1,000 US dollars.

Reform and opening up

The ten-year plan passed in 1990 intended to reform China and open the country up to the world. At this time the socialist market economy was enshrined in the statutes of the Chinese Communist Party and written into the constitution in 1993. This opening up led to the economic growth that meant improved living conditions for many Chinese people, but no adequate answers have been found to an unduly large number of questions relating to human rights problems. Nowhere in the world are the contrasts between poverty and prosperity, town and country, high-tech and natural conditions as marked as they are in China. And this ultra-rapid development still seems to be far from spent. Twenty-five years after the inception of the "reform and opening up" policy, China joined the World Trade Organization in 2001 and thus provided a further indication of how it is opening up to the world. A market of almost 1.3 billion people in an area of 9.6 million square kilometres is open to the world and looking for development and new standards in all spheres of life.

While the big cities have adopted and come up to Western standards, over 800 million people live in the country, of whom about 400 million are directly dependent on agriculture. The economic and social divide between the rural population in north-eastern, western and central China and the booming cities of the coastal regions has not remained unnoticed by the Chinese people and their government.

Social divide

On average, the urban population earns three times as much as the rural population. Industry and the service sector contribute over 50 per cent and 30 per cent respectively to the gross domestic product. Agriculture's share is about 15 per cent. The cities continue to become more attractive, while rural areas are keeping up with developments either with difficulty or not at all. Development programmes and tax concessions are intended to work against this, nevertheless many rural people see no future for themselves and there is huge migration to the cities. The enormous figure of about 130 million migrant workers makes its own contribution to urban growth. Labour is cheap, and the lack of modern machines and methods is balanced out by the never-ending influx of migrant workers. Even though it is not possible to reconcile the exploitation of these workers with the ideals of Chinese society, a blind eye is turned to the problem. There is no social security or medical care for migrant workers. Moreover, it is questionable whether foreign planners can influence this situation on their own building sites; as a rule, they affect the organization of the building process very little. It is clear from reports by architects on their experience of working in China that the quality of building project execution is not the only thing that suffers in this respect (see Chapter D, "Progress Reports").

Growth and "beacon projects"
The Chinese government is aggressive in its presentation of change and the opening up of China to the world. The Olympic Games in Beijing in 2008 and Expo 2010 in Shanghai are projects that symbolize this all too clearly, and they are celebrated as successes for the government's reform policy. In Beijing, work is currently under way on 20,000 building sites at the same time. Parks and green areas are to increase fourfold by 2008.

Shanghai has the fastest train in the world in the form of the Transrapid, one of the tallest buildings, the 492-metre-high Shanghai World Financial Center, one of the largest harbours and one of the largest airports. Building work for Expo 2010 is in full swing in the ultra-modern Pudong district.

Energy policy and its influence on the construction industry
Rapid growth in all spheres of the Chinese economy naturally also brings major problems in its wake. A few years ago energy consumption by the population, industry and buildings in general did not matter, but now energy supply and air pollution in the conurbations, along with rising costs, can no longer be ignored. For example, in 2004 the rise in energy consumption, about 15 per cent, exceeded the ultra-rapid 9.5 per cent economic growth. Chinese energy re-

quirements have risen by 65 per cent in the last three years alone. Considering the fact that about 67 per cent of the energy consumed in China is generated with coal, and the processes used fall far short of Western standards, it is easy to imagine the amount of pollution produced in the conurbations and the potential savings which will have to be exploited in the short or longer term.

In 2004, coal consumption worldwide rose by over 6 per cent, and two-thirds of this increase were produced by China. The declining exports of Chinese coal that this has brought about affect the global market price: along with other factors, in 2004 this led to a 69 per cent rise in the recommended European price for coal. Raw material prices for oil and steel, for example, are climbing rapidly all over the world.

The Chinese economy's energy and raw materials requirements cannot be covered by their own internal market. Entire steel production plants are being dismantled in Europe and re-assembled in China. How long can an economy cope with this ultra-rapid, non-sustainable growth?

The first steps are being taken to bring all this under control. The Chinese government is now insisting that the necessary energy-saving measures be taken for buildings. Energy-saving devices are being promoted for plants with high-energy consumption, and the growth of energy-intensive sectors is being restricted. These political initiatives are unambiguous and relate to the planning and construction market: the first move is that minimum standards have to be met for new housing and the enormous housing stock upgraded. New residential buildings and public buildings should use as little space and energy as possible. The Chinese Ministry of Construction now sees its principal task as being to promote structures that save energy and space as vigorously as possible. The entire economic system and popular awareness need to be shifted towards an informed and economical handling of energy. Processes and technologies that have long been standard in Europe and America are being introduced on the Chinese market: these range from fitting thermostatic controls for domestic heating systems to reusing waste heat in new ventilation and air-conditioning systems, using water-saving devices, and deploying environmentally friendly and energy-saving building materials.

Building clients are changing the way they think only slowly, but in the medium term they will have to. Meanwhile, implementing these new demands presents an opportunity for foreign planners and manufacturers of appropriate building products. Such expertise is presented and promoted at newly organized trade fairs and expert forums.

State-led measures

A 2 Changing Chinese architectural and building traditions

Dr Andreas Szesny

The change taking place in the overall shape of Chinese building and architecture around the turn of the century is the late product of a revolution. The historical changes in China's political and social spheres are now showing up in urban development and architecture, as the economic basis is now in place, in completely new and sometimes chaotic forms. Within a few decades, the urbanization rate in the world's most populous country will rise from just under 30 per cent at present to almost 50 per cent. Some of the background to this massive paradigm shift will be discussed below, to make it easier to understand what is currently happening in China.

The changes in thought and action for people in China have come about as a result of far-reaching historical events, and especially because of the "Great Chinese Cultural Revolution" between 1966 and 1976. While the 1968 movement was revolting in various ways against existing systems in Germany and other Western countries,

Ill. 2.1: A banner on an office building in Guangzhou saying "Develop China"

in China an embattled leaders' struggle for power, widespread weari-
ness with their own culture and the mixture of Chinese revolutionary
behaviour patterns with Western thought, especially in the form of
Marxism, culminated in a degree of iconoclasm that is unequalled
worldwide in the 20th century: the Chinese Cultural Revolution compelled older people to abandon their traditional values and, for a
decade at least, did not allow younger people a chance to acquire
them for themselves. A vast number of small shrines, house altars
and temples were destroyed and not reconstructed in this period.
The army was actually used to protect larger Chinese cultural assets
of major significance.

While the so-called Red Guard were carrying out onslaughts of
this kind, an attack was also mounted on the traditional structures
of general living accommodation and traditional town planning. This
was subtle and less directly aggressive and brutal, but it lasted far
longer, in fact from the 1950s to the present day. Above all, since the
1990s, when financial resources started to make it possible, China
has been experiencing a revolutionary aftershock in the field of architecture and the building industry. This has captivated architects
and planners in particular, just as the Cultural Revolution fascinated
some Western intellectuals at the time. Permission was finally given
for Rem Koolhaas's CCTV building in Beijing, not least to show the
world what the Chinese capital is now able to do: it can set new standards. China is no longer what it used to be. Thinking has changed,

Attack on traditional
living

Ill. 2.2: Luxury apartment buildings and Shell Museum on Xinghai Square in Dalian

and its architecture is following the same path. Here the question arises of what characterizes traditional Chinese architecture, and why was it abandoned?

A 2.1   Special features of traditional Chinese architecture

Traditional architectural influences

In historical China, architectural traditions were passed on only by word of mouth. Certainly architecture could reflect the building client's and the occupant's educational and social status, but planners and builders were not allowed any creative scope in this. *Feng shui* advisers could exert a certain amount of influence; they used different methods to present the way a building and its rooms should be aligned in relation to the surrounding energy flow. *Feng shui* experts increasingly practise today, after being discredited in the People's Republic for a time. Traditional ways of life, and thus also the functions surrounding them, were very deliberately abandoned after the Cultural Revolution. It is only since the 1990s, when attitudes started to revert to the country's traditions, that attempts have been made to use traditional Chinese elements again. This led to "blossom-style architecture": traditional roofs were no longer used on glass buildings for functional or religious reasons, but to create characteristic features that could identify a Chinese version of Modernism.

hutongs

Timber was the principal building material for centuries. *Hutongs*, the traditional courtyard dwellings, were the classical building form for accommodating the royal household and noble families. As a rule, as the important Chinese architecture historian Liang Sicheng shows, they used timber as the main building material, and beams as the main system. Wooden ox-head brackets serve as the ordering elements – *dougong* – combined with covered walks in the outside area, with additional rooms attached (see ill. 2.3). The special aesthetic quality is created by roof decorations on the covered walks, and by terraces, woodcarving, the choice of particular colours, the organization of the courtyards and thus a functional adaptation to the traditional Chinese way of life.

It is true that under the Han dynasty (206 BC – AD 220) stone started to be used to build tombs and ancestor temples, but this material was never accepted for general building use in traditional China.

The choice of material probably explains why traditionally no efforts are made to preserve original building stock. Sticking to timber construction meant that demolition and new building always took

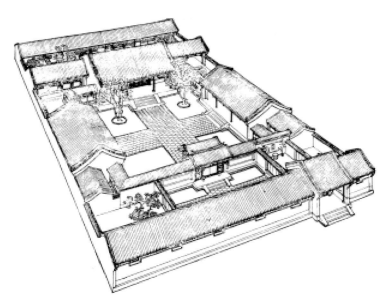

Ill. 2.3: Classical Chinese courtyard dwelling

place at points where a fresh start was made historically or after fires and natural disasters. Building activities in traditional China always derived from moral-philosophical ideas guided by traditional, Confucian conventions.

Timber is now used rarely or not at all for residential building. But it is the material that shaped the traditional and thus the culturally rooted treatment of architecture for centuries. For this reason, we can state that timber architecture and the traditional treatment of buildings have been mutually influential. As wood is not as long-lasting, the approach to architecture was different from that practised in Europe, for example. This was additionally reinforced by the interpretative framework of traditional Chinese thought, which saw cyclical change as the will of heaven. For this reason, it aimed more to find pragmatic solutions at the appropriate time, rather than looking for generally valid and irrefutable categories and expressing these in architectural form as well.

The very fact that the Chinese word for "town" – *chengshi* – begins with the character for "wall" shows that walls were a constitutive component of towns, quarters and courtyard dwellings placed at right angles. It was not the market place, but the political power centre that formed the core of a traditional Chinese town, whose functions were strictly regulated and built up around this "axis mundi".

Traditional city structure

Within this power base, the ruler celebrated the traditional ritu-als considered necessary to maintain harmony between heaven and earth, in tune with cyclical changes in the cosmos. All other func-tions were subordinated to this one, and arranged around the power base according to their significance. In such a stratified and strictly regulated society, everything and everybody had their precise place and prescribed function.

A 2.2   The background in terms of cultural history

People can often be seen in parks and public places in China writing their calligraphy on concrete surfaces. These characters are drawn in water, rather than ink, so they can be read only for a limited period as an expression of a particular state of mind, combined with the writer's technical ability. Only isolated writings by famous and learned rulers or holy men are placed in archives, given material form in stone, wood and paper and shown to the whole world in conspicuous locations. It is not the material itself that is the most valuable element here, but the description of the condition that it expresses.

Treatment of the housing stock

It is easier to understand the treatment of contemporary buildings with a useful life of 20 years against this background. When they are no longer fit to live in, they can be pulled down and replaced with new ones. Here we are not just talking about traditional resi-dential areas that have been there for over 50 or 100 years, but also about buildings dating from the 1960s and 1970s: concrete and brick structures erected when housing was urgently needed, pragmatically following the example of the Soviet Union for a time.

Change anchored traditionally

Transitions from one condition to another were systematically inves-tigated even in ancient China and described in the *Book of Changes – Yijing* – which is considered a Confucian classic. Phenomena of change could be captured this way in images, characters and hexa-grams. In present-day China, change is understood as something to be directed at specific targets, and instrumentalized appropriately. In contrast with earlier times, changes are no longer considered in cycles. Modern China often does not simply talk about "change" – *yi* – but about "development" – *fazhan*.

Demolition and development

Though it does not feature in the *Yijing*, the character for "demo-lition" – *chai* – is omnipresent in China today. It is used to define buildings whose occupants have to leave them shortly to make room

Ill. 2.4: Hotel extension in Qingdao (2006)

for "development". It is a matter of interpretation whether these are buildings appropriate to China's historical situation or whether the Cultural Revolution is being completed on the architectural plane. The *Book of Changes* was an aid to interpreting transformation and change that permeated Chinese thinking, but we can take the motto "development is the absolute principle", coined by Deng Xiaoping (the most influential politician and actual head of state in China from 1976 to 1997), as a propaganda call to accept change in the outward circumstances of life. It is, of course, understandable that most of those affected are at first delighted to move out of the backward conditions offered by cramped and dilapidated traditional residential areas into a two-bedroom flat with sanitary facilities and running water. However, new developments of traditional residential areas are not always approached sensitively, sometimes even with unemotional severity, and no consideration for occupants and developed structures. Such examples, where the understandable aim of creating new accommodation has overshot the mark through greed for profit, are in their own way late consequences of the Cultural Revolution.

Arguing from a different cultural angle, we are inclined to classify actions by protagonists in present-day China somewhere between pragmatic-and-adaptable and rash-and-irresponsible. The great architectural historian Liang Sicheng is said to have said "For my fellow-countrymen, architecture is like clothing". By this he meant that

Regular renewal

regularly renewing the building substance is foreseen within the functional context of traditional ways of thinking and living. This functional context was first challenged when Western colonial powers penetrated the country, questioned within Chinese society in the late 19th century and finally completely negated, above all at the time of the Cultural Revolution. Radical change of the complete social structure meant that architecture had to change as well: neither the substance nor the traditional functional background of the buildings was now seen as worth keeping. But another 30 years were to pass before the economic basis for widespread implementation made way for a fresh architectural start.

A 2.3   New structures for "outward appearance"

After the death of Mao Zedong and Hua Guofeng's transitional government, Deng Xiaoping, known as a pragmatist, took up the reins of Chinese government in 1978. Given the extensive measures resulting from the permanent state of revolution that had lasted for over a decade, Deng had a unique empire at his disposal: over a billion people who had just been subjected to the experiment of having all their traditional values deleted as if from a computer hard disk. Apart from the fact that historical memories cannot be expunged without difficulty, this represented an enormous opportunity to create something new.

Since the 1990s, China has been experiencing what are so far the greatest architectural changes in human history. They were launched by protagonists who, if they were between 45 and 65 years old in 1996 were between 15 and 35 in 1966, in other words at the beginning of the Cultural Revolution. These people were affected either actively as Red Guards, or passively as criticized class enemies. In retrospect, members of this generation are to be seen as victims by dint of the traumas they suffered, their lack of school education and the chaotic conditions that persisted for years. It is precisely the members of this generation who in the 1990s were placed in the position of being able to decide about the new face of China, at the same time as Jiang Zemin's "three representatives" campaign, which made the close alliance of political and economic power again acceptable.

xingxiang gongcheng

In 1992, in other words after Deng Xiaoping's southern tour of inspection, the so-called "outward appearance" or image project buildings – *xingxiang gongcheng* – were given a great boost. The party leader's positive appraisal of the city of Shenzhen spurred party

secretaries in all China's larger cities to imitate the new southern metropolis and create a favourable impression with their own
economic development. And in order to make this visible to all,
skyscrapers had to be built in places where experienced town planners would not necessarily have put them. Quite a number of projects
like this were in fact ultimately seen to have been mistakes, or the
developers ran out of money, often meaning that the shell was already complete and remained as an unused architectural ruin. After
the traditional values of moderation had been driven out of a whole
generation, it is hardly surprising that they temporarily lost their
sense of scale as well.

Ill. 2.5: Poster in front of the city hall saying "Just development is a consistent
principle", Qingdao (2006)

It has already been shown that traditional Chinese building stock
was of no particular value to most protagonists. Then we have the
well-preserved stone buildings, though from the Chinese point of
view these were built by imperialist aggressors, according to the
school books. But respect for the technical achievement and aesthet-
ics of the most important buildings is always present alongside rage
about this phase of Chinese history. Hybrids of Chinese and Western architecture, like *lilong* buildings in Shanghai or the two-storey
courtyard buildings with German-looking façades and tiled roofs in
Qingdao, are much more likely to be threatened with, or actually
face, demolition.

A 2.4   The role of foreign architects

Acceptance of Western
influences

The Chinese reformer Kang Yowei proposed over 100 years ago that
Western knowledge should be deployed within a characteristically
Chinese framework. It is only now that this is being practised on a
wider scale – an example of the time that many ideas take to seep
through. Western knowledge tended to be used against the will of
many Chinese in Kang's lifetime. And even the foreign architects who
shaped the image of Guangzhuo, Shanghai, Tianjin, Qingdao, Dalian,
Wuhan and other cities did not come because their Chinese hosts
wanted them to and invited them in. Thus the Chinese are always capable of seeing colonial architecture as a reminder of their own weak-
ness. Where this is no longer the case, it is evidence of new Chinese
self-confidence and their readiness to consider history objectively.

New ways of thinking
and realities

New self-confidence and a healthy need for recognition mean that
today Western architects are being invited to China in large numbers
to help build modern China. Fired by the planning possibilities and
supposed freedoms, a number of incredible visions are emerging, and
some are even realized. But many hopes have to yield to a series of
hard realities within the Chinese context. This easily leads to misunderstandings with a potential for triggering conflict. A tightrope
walk between personal ideas and interests, on the one hand, and
those of the client, on the other, defines each project. This includes
different ideas about finance, different aesthetic values, and differ-

Ill. 2.6: Building site for the opera house planned by Zaha Hadid in Guangzhou

ent ideas about quality and environmental protection. Foreign architects have to be careful not to seem like missionaries, but they must make sure that they are not simply exploited as mere providers of ideas.

The preference of Chinese homebuyers for south-facing dwellings is directly linked with traditional ideas. Climatic conditions alone do not seem to explain this adequately. Every architect commissioned to plan residential accommodation in China will have to confront expectations of this kind from the client sooner or later, even if that client originally asked for a modern, European, or even a German concept.

Fragments of traditional thinking in housing construction

The traditional expectation that buildings should be arranged looking from north to south continues unbroken. This idea of the best possible orientation is deeply anchored in the Chinese collective unconscious, and still determines homebuyers' approaches today.

A 2.5   The central axis

In the last century, China has broken with a thousand-year-old tradition of thought and rule that placed the emperor at the centre of everything that happened, along with the buildings from which he exercised his effective power as the son of heaven and link with the cosmos. This also applied in spatial terms, as the "axis mundi".

Since the unification of the empire by the first emperor Qin Shi Huang in the year 223 BC, the cities of Xi'an, Luoyang, Kaifeng, Hangzhou, Nanjing and Beijing have functioned as power centres, on average for not much longer than 350 years. At the end of the Chinese Civil War, when Mao Zedong proclaimed the People's Republic of China in Tiananmen Square, Beijing became the seat of government, after Chiang Kai-shek had ruled from Nanjing. This meant that the new rulers were killing two birds with one stone: firstly, it was possible to establish a physical distance from the old seat of government and its networks. Secondly, Mao and his Communist Party were taking advantage of the powerful symbolism of the former imperial palace, the Forbidden City: Mao took possession of the central axis of traditional Chinese power architecture and still dominates this today. His likeness is still in place, looking south over Tiananmen Square. The mausoleum containing his body stands in the middle of this square, on the central axis of power, as a place of pilgrimage for millions of visitors from all over China.

Centralization in Beijing

In the late 1950s, the Chinese architectural historian Liang Sicheng is said to have plucked up courage, raging and with tears in his eyes, to criticize Mao Zedong for his decision to pull down the old Beijing city wall, with the exception of one gate. He replaced it with a ring road that is now known in Beijing as the second ring, under which the underground also runs. If we ask ourselves today what lay behind Mao's decision, the following points emerge: first, the tendency to see the evidence and legacy of old Chinese culture as useless, or even obstructive and damaging; second, the tendency to cling on to local manifestations of the idea of centralized power through Tiananmen Square and the surrounding area. Mao did not want to open himself up to the idea of pitting other centres against Beijing as the historic centre, thus eliminating local comprehension of the centralized power notion, as adumbrated by the Cambridge-educated Liang. Russian advisers, who proposed modernizing the historic centre, were favoured, rather than the suggestion that Beijing should be decentralized, following European models.

Placing the Olympic Green in the northern part of Beijing's historical central axis suggests that this urban development decision is still linked with the traditional Chinese approach of placing buildings with religious or political significance on a north-south axis.

Decentralization in
other cities

In contrast with this, planning decisions have been taken in other Chinese cities in recent years that use decentralization or the shifting of a centre to make completely new developments in the town planning sphere possible. For example, the Chinese city of Guangzhou has just laid down a new urban axis so that the centre can be shifted by several kilometres. Hence the underground network can be developed and new modern developments carried out while at the same time leaving the old centre intact.

A similar decision was made about the city of Qingdao, where a new political and commercial centre was created as early as the late 1990s, as the only possible way of retaining the old town, with its characteristic colonial features.

Beijing also suffers from a series of transport policy decisions that were made too late, or wrongly. The underground network is too underdeveloped to take the load off the ring road system, so that life in Beijing is now subject to daily transport failure.

A 2.6   Pressure to adapt because of energy shortages

Energy shortage

It has been clear for years that China was heading for an energy crisis. In the past this idea was more or less ignored, or only received lip service. There are now regular power cuts and therefore production failures that could hit China very hard as a business location.

However, the recently passed 11th Five-Year Plan makes an about-turn, introducing extensive environmental protection measures for the first time, to be expressed at the German–Chinese level in the so-called Qingdao Initiative.

As maximum profits for investors and beautiful façades are currently still the most attractive factors in politicians' eyes, many new buildings use an unnecessarily large amount of energy. One example of a very recent project of this kind is the second Soho complex in Beijing: white cubes with no special heat insulation, attractive in urban development terms, simply glazed without protection against the sun, with high energy losses in both summer and winter. A young couple are basking in their reputation as avant-garde developers. They drew attention to themselves at the Beijing planning show by sponsoring and presenting a futuristic domestic kitchen designed by Zaha Hadid. One more example among many of careless energy handling is the new exhibition centre in Dalian: a smart glass palace that gets exhibitors and visitors sweating very quickly because no one thought about protection against the sun or sensible ventilation. It is idle to discuss whether this is the fault of the foreign architects, who normally pay better attention to such matters in their own countries, or the developers, who were far less thrifty in

Unnecessarily high energy consumption

Ill. 2.7: Protection against the sun in front of the glass façade of the new Dalian exhibition centre, but not on it

other respects. So far there have simply been no structures in place for implementing energy-saving measures across the board.

First moves against
wasted energy

The fact that 1.4 billion square metres of new housing will be built in China each year means that there is hope everywhere for change in this field.

People are paying attention to statements like the one made by Zhou Dadi, a representative of the National Development and Reform Commission, at a conference in Beijing: luxury should not be promoted, as for example in glass buildings that look wonderful but use distinctly more energy than others. Strictly speaking this also applies to many new airports and other structures, whether they are in Beijing, Shanghai, Guangzhou or other cities.

One exciting question remains open: how will Chinese society and its architecture respond to the pressure to adapt triggered by the energy shortage?

About the author:
Dr Andreas Szesny was born in Bielefeld in 1966 and studied in Munich, Taipei and Beijing. He has been following social, economic and architectural transformation processes in China at the closest possible range. At the time of writing he is directing a service centre for small and medium-sized businesses in the Chinese coastal town of Qingdao.

A 3 "Don't kill the dragon" – urban development in China

Matthias Wehrlin

China's economic, social and even cultural development is moving forward at a speed that is probably unique in history. Something that may be true today could be out of date by tomorrow. This report considers professional experience in the period from 1996–2005 and relates to urban situations. Given the size and geographical and cultural diversity of the Middle Kingdom, and the divide between town and country, it is hardly possible to make general statements. The conditions differ too much in this state, the most populous on earth, extending from Central Asia to the Pacific, from the north-east to the tropical regions in the border area with Vietnam, Laos and Myanmar. There are 25 different ethnic groups in the south-western province of Yunnan, for example.

The immediate juxtaposition of different cultures and states of development is an important feature of town planning, which has to organize a settled area that is expanding explosively, and is thus colliding with ways of life that have established themselves over decades and centuries. This country, which looks back over 5,000 years of history, is creating a new face for itself in the course of a few decades. An operation on a living and working body is proceeding at a unique pace.

A 3.1 Current urban development in China

About a quarter of a century has passed since the economic opening up under Deng. Economic growth is largely generated in cities, with a clear focus on the eastern megacities. Migration to the cities and increasing urban prosperity are leading to an exponential expansion in the need for per capita settlement area. Most Chinese cities are in a phase of extraordinary and historically unprecedented growth. As before, economic development axes and zones intended to serve heavy industry, manufacturing industry and the service sector are continuing to be provided.

Growth factors for settlement area requirements

In the relatively short period of economic upturn, the development perspectives have shifted fundamentally several times. Masterplans had to be continually adjusted to new horizons and larger scales.

Overlapping and sequence of concepts

Our Chinese partners have often surprised us with their long sight
and visionary approach in thought and action when they needed to
abandon outdated concepts in favour of ideas that could open up
new prospects both qualitatively and quantitatively. But this planning insecurity, along with the essentially unmanageable system of
different planning levels, planning instruments and responsible authorities, also means that ultimately decisions have to be taken arbitrarily, and there is no co-ordinated, agreed planning system.

The identity of urban
space

China's cities are undergoing an extraordinary and historically
unique phase of growth. The responsible authorities and the architects and planners they employ have to develop and make their
minds up about area strategies and urban development and architectural approaches extremely quickly. It is a particular challenge to
build cities, towns and quarters that are not only functionally adequate, but also offer identity, some unmistakable quality, and make
a positive emotional impact.

The gradual shift in economic direction and opening up that led
to the now well-known economic growth in recent years began under Deng in 1979. Although European architects also work in China,
the predominant influence is obviously that of American-style town
planning concepts. Evidence of this can be seen in area-intensive,
car-driven approaches directed at individual investment.

It is conceivable that the next historical development phase could
be the "Chinese age" (dynasty). A period of self-confident reflection
on their own traditions and values. It could be that urban spaces
and buildings are constructed again that have more to do with the
particular place, its people and their needs, than the faceless cities,
quarters and housing estates that are being realized in many places
at present. The fact that the remaining historic cities, such as Dali
or Lijiang in Yunnan province, for example, are proving such tourist
magnets shows that identity and moderation in scale are once more
in demand in modern Chinese society, and that the past is being
considered to a certain extent. Town planning has to make it a major priority to design housing that generates modern urban values
comparable with these historic cities.

Many of the current plans and projects seem very schematic, ran-
dom and repetitive. In contrast with this, cities that have grown
over the centuries, able to develop and renew themselves continually, are more complex and have a greater wealth of spatial and
functional features than cities that are produced out of thin air on
"greenfield" sites. Given that China is designing and realizing a lot
of housing, the need to integrate existing landscape, housing and
transport structures acquires particular significance. These "distur-

bances" can generate a certain complexity when overlaid with new structures. Linking new spatial elements with traces of local character enriches places and makes them distinctive. We followed this path of including local topographical factors and the existing settlement patterns and historical transport routes when designing the district of Wulong, part of Kunming's satellite town, Chenggong.

A 3.2   New space for the provincial capital Kunming

Kunming is the capital of Yunnan, a province in south-west China. China's southernmost province has over 40 million inhabitants and extends over several different climate zones. It includes tropical and subtropical areas on the borders with Myanmar, Laos and Vietnam, and also the foothills of the eastern Himalayan massif. Twenty-five ethnic minorities still live in this southern province. Kunming lies at about 2,000 metres above sea level. The city is near to the shallow

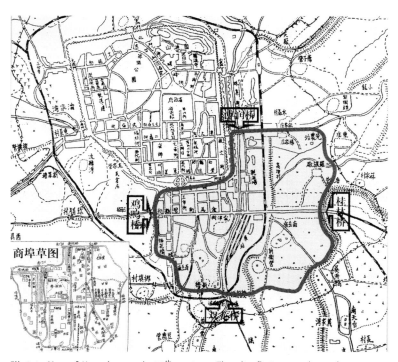

Ill. 3.1: Map of Kunming, early 20th century. The city first opened up when a commercial zone was established in 1905 in which foreign traders could also set up businesses. Even then Kunming was linked with Hanoi by a narrow-gauge railway built by the French colonial rulers.

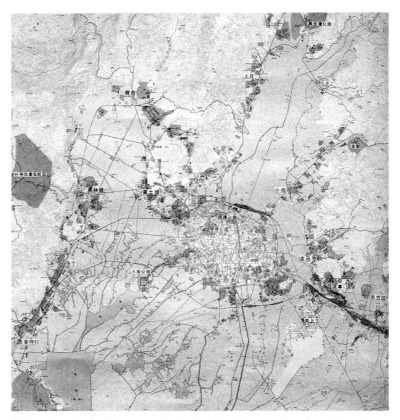

Ill. 3.2: Kunming is still a compact city in 1982. It is easy to make out the villages and industrial plants in a linear arrangement along the transport routes.

Lake Dian, which is about 40 kilometres long, and is surrounded by ranges of hills that set a limit on housing development. Kunming dates from the 8th century: in 743, Ge Loufeng, king of the Nanzhao Empire, visited the Kun prefecture and realized that the hills provided a protective background, while the plains between the hills could provide food for people.

The situation today: Kunming is separated from other competing cities of comparable significance by its topographical conditions. Guiyang, for example, the capital of Guizhou province, is 450 kilometres away. Kunming's strategically important position in the south of the Middle Kingdom has led to some significant infrastructure projects. The transport routes are to be enhanced as a prerequisite for future economic development. A new transport corridor consisting of a railway line and fast road to Myanmar, Bangkok and Hanoi is to be built; links with the major Chinese centres will also be up-

Ill. 3.3: 1987 development plan. A city with a diameter of about 8 to 10 kilometres is still being designed.

graded. Kunming is acquiring a new international airport that will also serve as a hub in future. Important logistics centres are being developed.

The Kunming urban area covers about 10,000 square kilometres and had about 3.2 million inhabitants in 1997. At that time the core city already had about two million inhabitants. While the population is declining in rural areas, it is assumed today that by 2020 Kunming itself will need to be able to house over seven million inhabitants. Here are a few pieces of information about recent planning history: the 1987 plan was based on a patchy city with a diameter of about 8 to 10 kilometres. Even by the mid 1990s it was clear that finger-shaped additional settlements in both the north and the south had to be zoned in. These two parts of the city are now largely built up. The city acquired a new look for the " '99 Kunming International Horticultural Exposition". Major new road axes

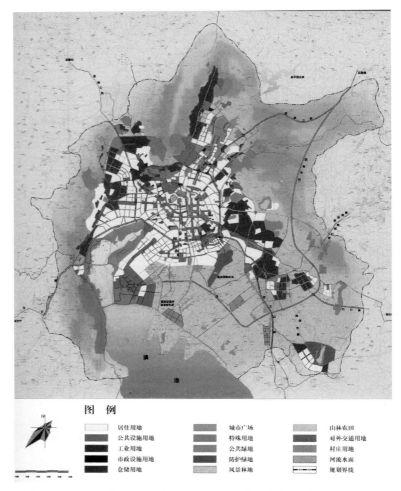

图 例

居住用地　城市广场　山林农田
公共设施用地　特殊用地　对外交通用地
工业用地　公共绿地　村庄用地
市政设施用地　防护绿地　河流水面
仓储用地　风景林地　规划界线

Ill. 3.4: Urban extensions were planned to the north and the south in 1996.

and parks were built, a lighting concept implemented and the first bus axis went into operation, developed with experts in the twin city, Zurich.

Today's conceptual framework is a development strategy aiming at an interlinked city structure with a radius of about 50 kilometres, whose core will be the urban system around Lake Dian. Three new towns are to come into being here. Chenggong will be the most important of the satellite towns, with 950,000 inhabitants.

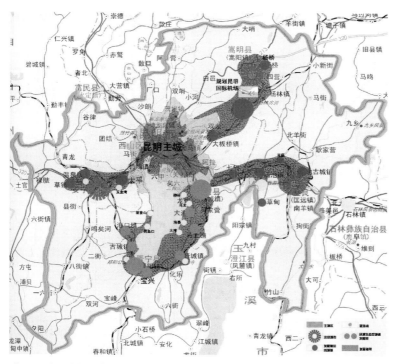

Ill. 3.5: The vision of an interlinked urban region with a radius of about 50 kilometres is accompanying Kunming into the 21st century.

A 3.3   The new city of Chenggong

Chenggong is immediately adjacent to the core city and is intended to offer space for up to ten universities working closely with the high-tech firms that are to be established here. Some of the city administration will be moved to Chenggong. A gigantic logistics centre and an international flower market offer jobs, as well as a development area intended for sport. High-quality residential areas will be built here in attractive locations on a slightly terraced site between the hills and Lake Dian. The 2004 Chenggong masterplan is based on the results of an international competition held in 2003. The urban area was divided up into seven planning perimeters for implementation and further concretization. These will be allotted to Chinese and international teams for further work.

Wulong – Black Dragon – will become a district of Chenggong. Wulong lies between the main axis of the new town of Chenggong and Lake Dian. The quarter covers 16.5 square kilometres and will house about 150,000 inhabitants. A large sports campus is the theme be-

Urban planning for the Wulong district of Chenggong

Ill. 3.6: Chenggong–Kunming masterplan showing the Wulong planning area (2004)

hind this district. The quarter adjacent to the north is devoted to
flowers, because the international flower market is sited there.

Our Swiss team worked as part of a joint venture with the Kunming Urban Planning and Design Institute (KUPDI), a former state
planning institute that has now been privatized. According to guidelines laid down in the 2004–2020 general masterplan, urban plans on
a scale of 1:5000 were to be produced within three months, and these
would then be revised as zoning, development, access and working
plans on a scale of 1:2000. Only two intermediate meetings were held
with the client, the Chenggong New Town Management Committee,
at the development stage.

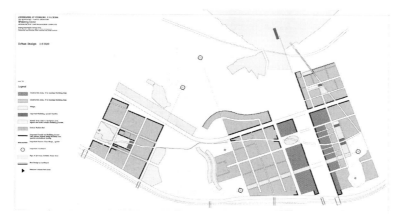

Ill. 3.7: Chenggong of Kunming, Wulong district. The urban concept on a scale of 1:5000 forms the basis for the individual development plans, which are drawn on a scale of 1:2000.

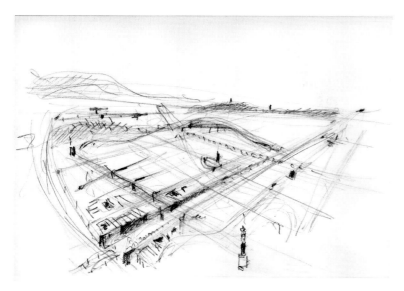

Ill. 3.8: The urban development concept defines the major spatial structures, but leaves a great deal of scope for architectural interpretation.

The following planning principles were laid down when work started: a defining spatial vision was to be devised for Wulong, creating appropriate conditions for developing a distinctive piece of city. Here the principles of sustainability and the urban development concept were of course to be respected.

Ill. 3.9: Situation for possible development

Urban development and
landscape concept

Maintaining and creating identity and spatial quality is at the heart
of the general urban development and landscape concept. For this
reason the spatial elements that identify a specific part of the terrain
as a special place should be retained and boosted. Here a crucial part
is played by the hills that structure the future urban space and offer
viewpoints. The line of hills to the south gave the area the name Wulong – Black Dragon. The now disused Chenggong airfield is built into
the design as a "landmark" and contributes to the place's unmistakable quality. The airfield was set up in the Second World War so that
China could have supplies delivered from India, a memorable part of

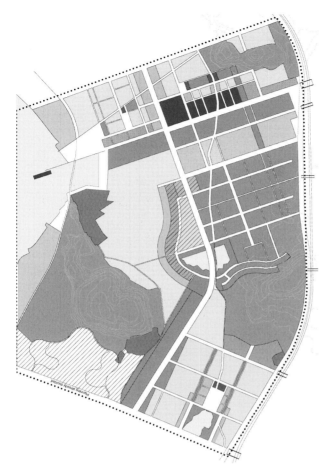

Ill. 3.10: Utilization plan 1:5000

China's turbulent recent history. In contrast with the essentially uni-
form masterplan, an attempt is made to clarify the polarity between
settlement, on the one hand, and landscape and water, on the other.
Settled areas were arranged in a more concentrated form. They are
juxtaposed with a coherent system of landscape, green spaces and
parks with different qualities. The road axes are subject to clear urban rules. The roads are part of the public space and subordinate
themselves to their function. The main axis is designed as a linear
park with little traffic, and links central Chenggong with Lake Dian.
The geometrical arrangement of the new road system is broken up by
traces of the historical road and route system. The old road linking
Chenggong with the south is an important landscape feature, and

should be integrated because it gives access to a large number of plots. This also makes phasing easier. Integrating other local connecting roads and agricultural cultivation routes can help to create identity and make it easier to understand the place. It is essential for such integration that the objects be suitable for the purposes of the planned new use.

All settlement edges are precisely defined. There are to be no "fraying" edges, just clearly formulated transitions from settlement to countryside that are also to be duly respected. The Wulong utilization concept proposes service, leisure and retail use on both sides of the main axis. The sports cluster includes training facilities, accommodation, therapy and wellness complexes and spectator facilities. Three residential areas are arranged around the centre of their respective quarters.

The development concept for the individual hills looks like this:

Wulong hill: the present "ecological desert" is being designed as a park with plants typical of the Yunnan locality. The viewing pagoda is precisely on the axis of an important road. A restaurant and other infrastructure are planned.
"Sport" hill: the freely accessible hill is to be afforested and is suitable for hiking, jogging, cycling, etc.
Chenggong hill: here a municipal park is to be created on a group of three hills that are already in part used for building; it will also include a viewing platform and a restaurant.

Access system

Two tram routes linked to the new Chenggong main station and that can be used as BRT (Bus Rapid Transport) in the first development phase form the spine of the public transport access system. Full bus access is planned for the entire area. The internal transport network will be relieved by a new road that will run parallel with the motorway. Direct slow transport networks and road profiles permitting safe crossing are important elements of the transport concept.

A 3.4 Experiences

The radical nature of the approach to development in Chinese cities is impressive. Being receptive to new ideas, international exchange of ideas and concepts and use of international urban development competitions is now taken for granted. The level of professionalism has increased considerably within a short period.

Those responsible politically and administratively, and the planners, are under enormous time pressure in face of the demand for

Ill. 3.11: Photograph of Chenggong

new accommodation. The changeable history of the 20th century has meant that a new generation has to design, decide about and realize concepts from nothing, as it were, without having recourse to a tradition comparable with Western Europe. This often results in a certain eclecticism. International models, above all from the Anglo-Saxon countries, are taken over directly, without reflecting about the local climatic, topographical and cultural situation, or about settlement history. This means that towns and parts of towns come into being that are randomly interchangeable.

There is no coherent, binding planning system today. The interplay of overriding masterplans, local utilization and development plans, and concrete building and infrastructure projects is opaque. There also seem to be no binding guidelines and standards. For complex projects, like the new Chenggong station, there is a lack of experience in dealing with effective project organizations covering several institutions.

Finally, let us go back to the title of this section. In summer 2001 I had the opportunity to draw up the masterplan for the Pukou Campus of Nanjing University with professors, and also other experts from the Nanjing University Institute of Architecture. The site lay beyond the Yangtze River, on the edge of a plain, embedded in the foothills of a range. During the discussions I, too, had derived design ideas from *feng shui* principles. When I deviated from the principles in one case and wanted to "sacrifice" a little hill from the lower re-

"Don't kill the dragon"

gions of the formation, I was directly confronted with the rules I had brought into play: "Don't kill the dragon". *Feng shui* is now back on the town planning agenda. We, too, turn to it for our town planning designs, and our Chinese partners understand us.

About the author:
Matthias Wehrlin is a freelance town planner in Bern. He works mainly in Switzer-land and occasionally also in France, Germany and Austria. He has worked within the Zurich–Kunming twinning since 1996. He now looks after other projects in the Yunnan and Jiangsu provinces.

The framework for building in China

B 1 Project control in China

Hans-Peter Holler

B 1.1 Legal bases

The Chinese building industry is on its way to becoming one of the most highly regulated sectors. Even though there is nowhere near as much monitoring and control as in telecommunications, for example, a bewilderingly large number of laws, procedures, approval procedures and tests relating to erecting and running buildings have to be taken into account in the property sphere. Engineers, architects, consultants, experts and building companies must be able to produce a certificate of competency in their specialist area. A certificate defines the precise scope of the relevant services, and also the size and degree of difficulty of projects it is permissible to work on. Project management services were not placed on a legal footing until late 2004. In the meantime the Ministry of Construction has issued a provisional law, called the *Construction Project Management Provisional Measures*. These *Provisional Measures* put project management regulation on a formal basis, and came into force on 1 February 2004.

In many countries project management is a wide-ranging field including a number of different professional fields and services. Hitherto, attempting to place these services in a legal framework had seemed impossible. Project management was regulated by applying contract law, rather then by using normative regulations.

The *Interim Measures* apply to all project management services relating to building projects where a developer has brought in a third company to provide professional management and consultancy services. They also cover a series of activities that support the developer in his work:

Services covered by *Construction Project Management – Interim Measures*

- project development, financial viability studies, investment
- location studies, planning and planning permission requirements
- preparing planning requirements, organizing competitions and assessing competition results, issuing invitations to tender for planning services and planning checks, setting up and monitoring planning contracts, involvement in optimizing final planning
- involvement in issuing invitations to tender for site supervision services

- involvement in issuing invitations to tender for construction services
- involvement in monitoring construction services and controlling deadlines, costs and quality
- involvement in acceptance, takeover and start-up

This list shows that project management covers the whole construction process cycle, starting with supporting project development, via financial viability studies, invitations to tender and awards to monitoring planning and building services and start-up. Every company providing services from this catalogue, whether from China or abroad, is subject to the *Interim Measures* regulations. Hitherto no special qualification had been required for project management services. There is still no state office that issues a project management certificate.

The *Provisional Measures* now require project management firms to prove they are qualified in one or more of the services fields listed below:

- consultancy
- planning
- execution of construction work
- site supervision
- cost planning
- invitation to tender and tender awards

This means that all management companies must be in possession of one or more of these qualification certificates.

The *Provisional Measures* also insist that the project manager be independent. Links with construction firms involved in the project are not permitted. Conflicts of interest between the client and the planning and realizing firms are thus to be avoided. The project manager is commissioned by and works in the interests of the client.

The *Provisional Measures* lay down that project management services fees are negotiable. It is also possible to agree to work on the basis of an agreed savings percentage achieved by project management through particular measures or proposals.

Introducing the *Provisional Measures* creates a danger that professional project management is not seen as an essential requirement in China. It also implies that it would be sufficient to become a project manager to book a course, learn rules and finally pass an examination. This type of project manager would certainly master all the theories, but would have little experience in putting these theories into practice in day-to-day project management.

Project management services for construction projects are still not widely available in China. Professional project management is essentially offered by foreign companies. Traditionally in China, organizing planning, invitations to tender, tender awards and project realization is in the hand of the design institutes, on the one hand, and the project development and main contractors, on the other. Chinese site supervision companies increasingly try to offer project management services as well. Project management departments have also come into being in the large Chinese project development and construction companies. These departments are now being transformed into independent project management firms. The Ministry of Construction (MOC) is aggressively campaigning for the introduction of project management services in the building sector.

Project management in China

In 2003, the MOC published a recommendation to promote contract management and project management development. In order to advance Chinese firms rapidly and effectively in this way, it was obvious that internationally accepted procedures should simply be adopted for project management.

In the context of these measures, the MOC published the *Code of Management of General Project Contracting* for building projects in August 2004. This recommendation is fundamentally a national standard and defines matters including standards for project management, scheduling, cost planning, quality and safety management and contract management.

The introduction of this recommendation is another step that creates a basis for realizing complex projects successfully within the scheduling and cost framework, while at the same time maintaining quality standards.

B 1.2   Project development

Apart from government investment, international capital plays an important part in the Chinese property market. The field is dominated by investors from Hong Kong, Taiwan and Singapore. Investors and project developers are mainly interested in creating high-quality office space, exclusive apartments and detached houses, and shopping centres, the types that promise the highest profits.

Investors

Town planning departments influence land distribution; they simultaneously administer and participate in the land distribution and planning process. Now that the land use system has been reformed, leasing plots of land has become an important source of income. While the municipal government promotes investment conditions, it is involved in project developments itself, using its own capital re-

Land Use Law

sources, through the state property companies. This means that the municipal government, on the basis of its own interests, responsibilities and powers of instruction, can compel the planning department to allow concessions relating to planning principles. Project developers and investors who want to invest in a market with fair competition conditions are scared off by the municipal government's powerful position and the possibly corrupt behaviour this implies. Regulations about the nature and scope of building use are often altered by influence.

The Land Use Laws have a time limit between 40 and 70 years according to the type of use:

- trade   40 years
- industry   50 years
- residential   70 years

Three administrative departments are involved in plot distribution: the administrative planning, town planning and land administration departments.

The administrative planning department has the dominant role among these departments. It determines the nature of a plot and the extent to which it can be used for building on the basis of a development plan. An application for permission to use a plot must be submitted to the administrative planning department. After receiving planning permission, another land use application is submitted to the land administration department. As a government department, this institution is responsible for requisitioning the land from the

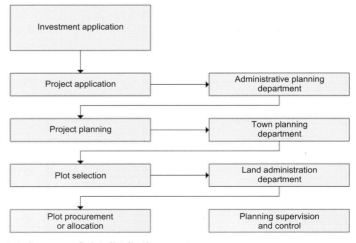

Ill. 1.1: Sequence of plot distribution events

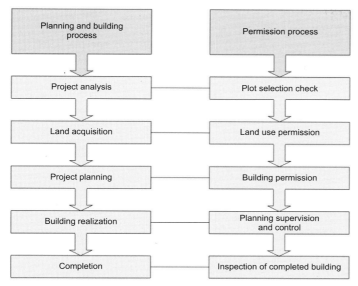

Ill. 1.2: Planning and authorization process

former plot user. But the plot always remains state property. It is possible to own the building itself (offices and dwellings).

The building authorization process runs in parallel with the use permission process. The functions of the government departments involved are interlinked. Project developers and the town planning and land administration departments often have different interests.

Building permission

To receive final planning permission, numerous conditions, some of them contradictory, laid down by the administrative departments must be met. Bureaucratic obstacles lead to delay and additional expense.

Contacts with authorization offices take place on three levels:

Level 1   Mayor, deputy mayor, deputy party secretary
Level 2   Authorizing authorities
Level 3   Contacts via design institutes and entrepreneur

Regional and local planning and land use requirements must be heeded when accessing building land. Planning permission is sought from the authorities before the project begins. Construction completion and checking documents and acceptance documents are applied for when building is completed. Here, documents are required from at least ten administrative bodies, including fire protection, quality control, safety, hygiene, etc. They are then submitted to the building authority to be checked and approved. The building authority can

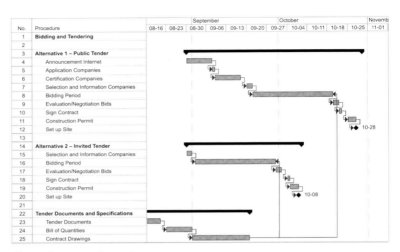

Ill. 1.3: Sequence of award events

then order modifications. If no ban on use is issued within 15 days, permission to use is considered granted.

Invitation to tender and tender awards
There is a duty to issue public invitations to tender, which is organized by a tendering agent, for projects of public interest (e.g. infrastructure) or projects wholly or partly financed from state funds and other state-financed projects (e.g. Chinese-foreign joint ventures) (see also Chapter B 2.2).

There is a special version known as a limited tender invitation requiring permission. Here bidders can be chosen and influence can be exerted on the composition of the award committee. This process is admissible for joint venture projects.

Public invitations to tender based on bills of quantities are carried out by tendering agents against a fee. These offices decide which firms will be invited to tender, send out tendering documents, assess the bids and come to a decision about which firm will be awarded the contract on the basis of fixed assessment criteria.

Although the Chinese authorities have often tried to impose it, wholly owned companies are not obliged to invite to public tender. For this reason, foreign developers prefer to control the invitation to tender and award process themselves. In this way awards can be granted to firms who are in the best position to realize the project in conformity with the planning, scheduling and quality requirements.

B 1.3 Planning and building realization

There are about 2,000 design institutes in the Chinese building in-dustry and they play a key part. With respect to planning tasks, they are comparable with German architectural and planning prac-tices, but their power is considerably greater, as they are responsible for more aspects of the planning process:

Design institutes

- architect services
- structural engineering
- civil engineering
- soil investigation
- technical building equipment
- landscape planning
- spatial development

Fundamental differences from Western institutions are the involve-ment with state institutions and commissioning bodies whose firms employ from 1,000 to 2,000 people, and involvement with companies in the building materials and building industries, connections that are forbidden in Germany and Europe. In China some subsidiaries of the design institutes have a 50 per cent market share, as the insti-tutes are involved in all planning processes, and can make decisions about materials, for example. The institutes influence tendering pro-cesses to an equal extent.

No main contractor services (design-and-build services) are put out to tender in China. The design institutes have a monopoly in the planning field. Chinese building firms usually lack the planning experience that firms in Europe or the USA usually have. In Ger-many the HOAI (Regulations on architects' and engineers' fees) de-fines the planning levels for the individual planning phases (phases one to five), but Chinese planning is based on building catalogues – *guobiao* – containing standardized planning and details. The design institutes copy the foreign planners' procedures. They use standard details and CAD programs to draw up final construction plans.

The central government requires design institutes to provide all planning and engineering services for projects of a certain size and larger. This includes design planning, permission planning and the final building plans and tendering documents.

Design institutes are state enterprises. Planning quality differs greatly from institute to institute and some institutes do not con-form with customary international standards. For foreign developers in particular, the design institutes exert considerable influence over building costs, scheduling and quality. The institutes are graded from

A–D (see also Chapter B 2.2.5 Architecture and engineering contracts).

Building firms

Main and general contractors also appear as specialist firms for certain trades in the Chinese building industry.

Building firms fall into three ownership categories:

- *state-owned enterprises directly controlled by the state financial planning body*. These firms are well equipped and able to execute complex building procedures.
- *building enterprises owned by state collectives*. These companies are run by a collective and not attached to the ministry directly, but in fact they are state companies. Provinces and local authorities have local companies (holdings) that report directly to the local building commission. The role of these companies is to co-ordinate a series of building firms and building material manufacturers.
- *building enterprises owned by genuine collectives*. The genuine collective enterprises work in rural areas and are managed by towns and neighbourhood committees.

Like the design institutes, the building firms also have to have certain licences and are divided into three classes. This classification determines the nature and size of the projects they are allowed to carry out. The criteria are investment levels, experience and references.

The *China State Engineering Corporation (CSEC)* outstrips all other enterprises in the building industry in terms of turnover and number of employees. The company is divided into 50 individual building firms and has a total of up to 190,000 employees.

B 1.4   Project management in practice

Fundamentals

This analysis will not attempt a theoretical study of project control and project management services. There is extensive specialist literature on this subject. But the following is indispensable for a successful project manager, in China as well:

- he must be able to work with other people without holding any prejudices
- he must have clear ideas about how planning and building processes work
- he needs fully developed expert systems and experience
- he must be accepted as co-ordinator by all those involved

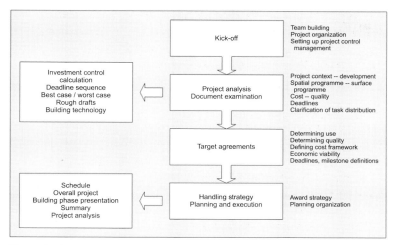

Ill. 1.4: Project sequence structures

If the process is to be correctly structured, the project manager must give due consideration to the needs of all those involved. If this basic rule is ignored, it is highly unlikely that the project participants will be prepared to cooperate constructively, especially if they come from different cultures.

Aims of project control

This is based on detailed analysis of the client's ideas and requirements. Here requirements relating to function, construction and finishing should be examined in detail and matched to each other. Those involved should decide at an early stage which materials or equipment will have to be imported. Delivery periods, logistics and import regulations must be considered when scheduling. Alternatively, Chinese-made joint-venture products or local materials and equipment can be procured. In this case time must be allowed for quality and cost comparisons and for evaluating references supplied.

Project sequence strategy

The decision about whether materials are to be imported or procured locally has a considerable influence on the cost framework. Particular heed should be paid to selecting suitable materials and to attention to detail. Planning requirements must be matched to the design institute's and the local building firms' ability to deal with them efficiently. Good coordination between the foreign planners and the design institute is essential if planning and building are to proceed smoothly.

Deploying sufficient capacity tends to be of secondary importance to the building process: it is more important to ensure that sufficient qualified supervision staff are employed on the building site.

Untrained migrant workers are often employed, and there is a lack of skilled use and careful handling of building materials and of attention to quality. Efficiency and quality, and the standard of the machinery in the factories, must be examined when choosing subcontractors for specialist services involving a high degree of prefabrication (steel erection, façade, services). As well as controlling the flow of building events, the prescribed site supervision plays an essential role. Here project management commitment is an additional requirement. Using project managers with practical experience offers support when coordinating individual processes, monitors the quality of execution and meeting material and planning requirements, and establishes coordination between building and technical trades. For large, complex projects it makes sense to have an additional construction manager permanently present on the building site.

Project organization   The best possible buildings are created by defining aims clearly, planning creatively and managing processes professionally. Friction losses can be reduced, quality created and time and money saved by "imposing order" and "doing the right thing at the right time".

To sum up: if a project is to run successfully, project management should address the following matters:

– building up the project structure, contracting (support from project control)
– defining the aims, purpose and scope of the building project
– making and recording decisions (preparation through project control)
– securing the ability to acquire permissions (support through project control, cooperation with Chinese partners with good contacts with the authorities)
– monitoring scheduling, cost and quality targets (implementation through project control)

It is crucial when carrying out projects in China that an independent project controller is put in place to support the client in respect of project management. The controller must, in the higher interests of the client, ensure that the project is coordinated and runs to schedule, that cost targets are met, and he must support the project management in preparing decisions and other client-related tasks. Project control should be based on direct relationship to overall project management, on a line-management or staff basis. In the case of line-management, the project control team is empowered to issue instructions to project participants, wherever they apply to measures relevant to the progress of the work or cost. On a staff basis, the project control team prepare documents and recommen-

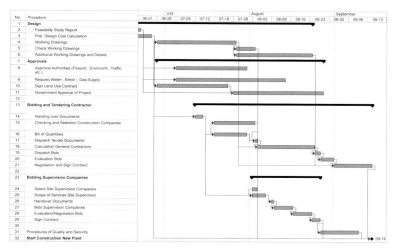

Ill. 1.5: Schedule for the planning and preparation phase

dations which are then implemented by the client's project management team.

Any decision about a building plot must be preceded by exhaustive local and regional research, and market and location analysis. This also includes assessing the topography and the subsoil situation, both factors that affect building costs considerably. In the case of industrial projects, there will often be several industrial parks in direct competition. To avoid conflicts of interest, local planning practices should not be involved in the selection phase as a matter of principle.

Plot selection

It is very important to define project aims. Organization concepts, development concepts and design requirements are summed up in a physical and function programme. The physical programme lays down detailed guidelines on land use and function areas, including statements on unit spacing, room dimensions, and the height of rooms and storeys. Process flow and production logistics have to be fixed for industrial projects.

Programming

For Chinese projects, the preliminary planning at least should be in the hands of the foreign practice, and the Chinese planning practice will draw up the design and working plans subsequently. It is better, but also more expensive in terms of time and cost, for the foreign practice to draw up a full design plan as well. This will include drawings of the building in ground plan, section, elevations and key details, technical descriptions stating standards for the building and services, and all-important schemes. As well as this, system planning can define a financial planning concept for the building's technical

Preliminary planning to design planning (system planning)

services. Reducing energy consumption and emissions is becoming increasingly important in China. Innovative solutions can be built into the planning process.

Alternatively, a *"design-and-build"* model can be chosen: a main contractor is commissioned to plan and realize the building. In this case international building firms will have to be used, as Chinese firms do not offer planning services as a rule.

Choosing the planning practice

Choosing a suitable planning practice is extremely important. Introducing a pre-qualification process provides essential insights about efficiency, specialist knowledge and quality: three to five applicants receive preliminary design documents and the building programme. Then interviews are held, reference evidence examined and the practices visited on the spot. But the key features are planning quality, knowledge of materials, degree of detail, and CAD and office equipment. The ability to coordinate building and technical planning is particularly relevant.

Design and authorization planning

Coordination and control of the planning process and content are particularly important in this planning phase. In no circumstances should planning in China be left to the design institute alone. Regular planning and coordination meetings examine the planning process in its entirety to ensure that guidelines and standards are being met. It is important to coordinate routing and to check for collision points.

Working plans

Regular coordination, control and support are also required at the final planning stage. Coordinating building and technical workers within the planning team is often a weak point as well. Important details and technical specifications have to be demanded. It is not usual in China to present details on a scale of 1:20 to 1:5, and these planning features have to be insisted on; a great deal of convincing argument will be needed.

Invitation to tender and tender awards

Tender documents drawn up to Chinese standards are less detailed than comparable Western tender documents. Considerable importance should be attached to detailed working drawings. Drawings should be ranked before tender documents. It is not permissible to insist on specific product makes. Materials must be described neutrally in terms of product. This means that the building firm is able to use inferior materials without the client's agreement. This often results in buildings with serious deficiencies in quality and execution. To avoid these negative consequences, architects try to go beyond the standard guidelines to prevent the use of inferior quality materials. Also, Chinese planning and industrial standards are antiquated and do not yet meet national or international standards.

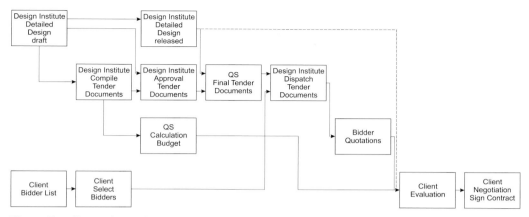

Ill. 1.6: Flow diagram for tender invitation and award

As a rule, five to ten firms (general contractors or firms offering individual services) are invited to tender. Often foreign firms with branches in China are invited as well. Bids from such firms come out well above those of their Chinese competitors.

After the bids have been evaluated, negotiations are conducted with the most reasonable bidders. Awards are decided on the basis of reference projects, quality of execution and evaluations of special proposals. Because the subsoil is so poor, the use of deep foundations on alluvial land is widespread. To gain time, the underground engineering work can be put out to earlier tender and award to specialist building firms.

The legislation requires using local site supervision and a quantity surveyor (see Chapter B 2.2). Site supervision requirements are not the same as the standard German site supervision requirements laid down in HOAI, Phase 8. Chinese site supervision practices offer the following service pattern under the headings "quality monitoring" and "safety management": Building and completion phase

- examining the working plans
- quality control for building materials
- quality control for building plant and equipment
- building site safety
- checking current building progress
- examining the qualifications of the building site personnel
- demanding and examining inventory documents

Only building sites that also convey an impression of an orderly approach can produce quality and work effectively. This includes cleanliness and safety. Chinese building sites need pioneering work in this field. It does not make any sense to compel the contractor to adopt a particular working programme that runs counter to his own ideas. It is in fact advisable to make concessions in order to make best use of the available production and fitting methods. Quality control starts even in the planning phase. In the actual building phase, care should be taken to ensure that the required materials are really used, and that product-specific fitting requirements are met.

The contractor can make alternative proposals to the tender standards. These are examined and approved on the basis of specimens and references.

It has turned out to be worthwhile to build specimen rooms before the actual building phase starts, to test the guidelines for details and materials and introduce improvements to materials and details in good time. It is essential to check and approve the quality of finish in the form of mock-ups before production begins for façades, roof areas and other critical parts of the building.

The quality control process ends with the correction of faults and the start-up phase. Buildings are officially accepted in China at the point of *final acceptance*. The quality bureau, the fire prevention department and the environmental health office have to approve in order to ensure successful acceptance. The as-complete plans should be drawn up by the planning practice, as the building firm usually delivers these too late, and in poor quality.

Documentation

Communication

It is a characteristic feature of Chinese building projects that a large number of participants have to work together, under pressure from deadlines and cost factors, on the basis of differing information from various locations. This creates the necessity for a "digital platform" that gives those involved in the project access to up-to-date documents and the ability to communicate with the same aims in mind and to keep up with the work as it needs to be done. But the project management team should have access to central scheduling and work monitoring, including reporting. These systems link those involved in the project, control the workflow, and distribute news, documents and information.

B 1.5 Planning and building costs

Quantity surveying

Chinese quantity surveyors provide the same services as their English model. Quantity surveying is the generic term for cost planning and cost control. Quantity surveying includes tender award and contract management, both of which are part of the cost control process. The quantity surveyor is commissioned by the client directly and assists with planning and controlling project investment. He represents the client's financial interests throughout the entire course of the project. During the realization phase the quantity surveyor evaluates the level of work completed so that part-payments and supplementary demands can be fixed, assists in warding off complaints, or evaluates and negotiates with the company over justifiable additional demands. Effective cost control is carried out within the project management framework. All the costings are noted in a cost monitoring system. Cost monitoring is not a passive system. Precise project control means that cost changes can be identified even in the initial phase. Causes and effects of measures affecting costs are conveyed to the project management team at an early stage so that counter-measures can be introduced where necessary.

Cost reduction opportunities are largely exhausted by the end of the planning phase. The diagram in ill. 1.7 shows where opportunities to influence project flow occur.

The diagram makes it clear that realization decisions made in the early planning phases crucially influence fixing the cost framework. The importance of control increases when planning is concluded and during the realization phase.

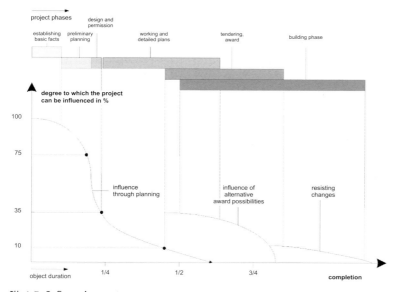

Ill. 1.7: Influencing costs

Despite the overwhelming volume of investment by Western standards, professional cost and schedule control rarely occurs in China. Moreover, clients who are commercially successful and put a great deal of money into building projects often have no knowledge of how to implement and control planning and building work, and often rely on their experience in other industries. Even though the predominant Chinese enterprise culture is not comparable with the Western world, professional project management will be indispensable in future if building investment is to accomplish its aims.

About the author:
Hans-Peter Holler has been responsible, as managing director of Drees & Sommer Ding Shanghai, for China and the Asia-Pacific area since 2004. He has worked for Drees & Sommer since 1974. From 1982–1984 he was in Zanzibar to advise on planning and running various building projects for the German Development Service. From 1995 to 1999 Hans-Peter Holler was overall project manager responsible for the DaimlerChrysler "Potsdamer Platz" project. In 1999 he became a member of the Drees & Sommer Berlin management board and managing director of the Drees & Sommer / Kohlbecker Gesamtplan GmbH. In this function he was in charge of various new embassy building projects, rebuilding the Olympic Stadium in Berlin and a new Formula 1 racetrack.

B 2   Building Law in China

RA Dr Christian Gloyer

B 2.1   Introduction

China is an alien world for Europeans and Americans in particular. This does not just apply to culture: legal perceptions and legal practice in China are also very different. The central legal concept, *fa* in Chinese, means both "law" and also "method" or "way". The word for law in the sense of a personal legal right – *quanli* – is made up of a component meaning "power" and one that can be translated by "benefit" or "profit". Even here it can be seen that the Chinese concept of law is not as rigid as the European one. Laws are to be understood as methods and guidelines for state power, and rights as advantageous, but not necessarily inalienable, positions of influence and power.

The legal system of the People's Republic of China

The People's Republic of China calls itself a *socialist constitutional state* in the preamble to its constitution. This means that all state organizations on all levels are obliged to abide by the constitution and the law (Article 5 of the constitution). The constitution further expressly guarantees protection of the *legal rights and interests* of foreign companies working in China.

Socialist constitutional state

Essentially the term "socialist constitutional state" means two things: the constitution itself provides for a socialist-style property law. One of its provisions is that land in cities and all mineral resources belong to the state authorities. A twin-track concept applies to ownership of the means of production: on the one hand public ownership of the means of production is pre-eminent, to prevent capitalistic exploitation of human beings by human beings; on the other, however, a complementary sector of rural and urban private economy is accepted (under Articles 6–11 of the constitution). Legal private ownership is guaranteed and protected under the constitution, expropriation is admissible and subject to compensation only within legal limits and for the general good.

The adjective "socialist" further implies that law in China remains bound to the aim of achieving Communism under the leadership of the Chinese Communist Party (CCP) and in compliance with Marxism-Leninism and the ideas of Mao Zedong as well as the theories of Deng Xiaoping.

Legal standards versus Party standards

As has already been mentioned, the concept of law in Chinese is more ambiguous than in German or European linguistic usage. Law always implies methods as well, and that suggests a means to an end. So the term *standard* would actually be closer to the Chinese *fa*.

The distinction between *legal standards* and *Party standards* is very important in Chinese legal practice. The latter are political guidelines laid down by the CCP and its committees, and they may also contain requirements for certain economic sectors. These Party standards – and this absolutely contradicts Western constitutional state traditions – take precedence over constitutional law in cases of conflict.

Generally accessible and internal standards

It is important to distinguish between *external*, i.e. publicly accessible or published standards, and *internal – neibu –* standards intended for domestic use by the Chinese organs of administration. Internal standards can, for example, guide the discretion of the responsible officials when approving a project involving foreign participation. Even though it is said that the significance of internal standards has noticeably declined in recent years, especially after China joined the WTO, this instrument used by the Chinese administration for centuries is nevertheless still deployed, and should be considered as an uncertainty factor for foreign investors in China.

Local regulations and practices

It should be noted that the 22 provinces of China, five autonomous regions and four cities under the direct jurisdiction of the central level, China's highest level of government, Beijing, Shanghai, Tianjin and Chongqing, are all able to issue their own regulations in most spheres relevant to developers and planners. These may not contradict the laws and regulations made at the central level, but in practice it is not unusual for deliberate or accidental deviations of this kind from the Beijing rules to crop up. Foreign businessmen should also keep their eye on the way local authorities handle certain laws. Considerable differences can occur from town to town and from region to region.

Legal system

The Chinese legal system is still in considerable need of reform. Faced with rapid economic change and an increasingly open and liberalized society, there is a growing need in China for reliable justice that can also tackle the complicated manifestations of a modern market economy. Problems arise here, above all, from inadequate training for judges, and partly also from the legal profession. In the past, Party functionaries or military men were often made judges without any legal training, after the country's legal faculties had been closed down at the height of the Cultural Revolution. These judges sometimes cannot cope, particularly in complex cases, and pronounce judgments that do not even conform with Chinese law, never mind the sense of law felt by the foreign developers affected.

There is no doubt that corruption is a weak point among Chinese officials and judges; such behaviour is officially defined as "local protectionism", i.e. the considerable inclination shown by state offices to favour local people over strangers and Chinese people to foreigners generally. The judges are usually better trained in the two metropolises, Beijing and Shanghai, and probably less prone to corruption and local protectionism than in the hinterland; these, too, are circumstances that should not be underestimated when choosing a location.

Corruption

Chinese Civil Law is essentially Continental-European in character. The great German legal edifices, above all the Bürgerliches Gesetzbuch (BGB, the German Civil Code), have exercised considerable influence, in a roundabout way via Russia. This basis was present anyway, but it has been developed through cooperation in various ways between German and Chinese institutions, such as, for example, the Gesellschaft für Technische Zusammenarbeit (GTZ: Society for Technical Cooperation) or the German Patent Office, over the last few years and decades, so that German legal practitioners can find their way about Chinese legal systematics very well.

Civil Law

The following relevant Chinese civil legislation is also important for foreigners in China – with no claim to completeness:

- general principles of Civil Law
- Contract Law
- Law of Civil Procedure
- Social Law
- Foreign Trade Law
- Labour Law
- insolvency legislation

The *General principles of Civil Law* (1987) contain a great deal that is laid down in the German Civil Code (BGB). But there are a large number of gaps, particularly in Contract Law, and the approach certainly does not correspond with current Chinese legislation technique. Chinese legislators have recognized that this law needs to be reformed, and have been preparing a book of Civil Law for several years.

General principles of
Civil Law

The *Contract Act* (1999) has 428 paragraphs containing obligatory legislation, about the form and compilation of contracts, for example. Some modern contract types have also been incorporated in this

Contract Law

law, and these are essential for the building industry; as well as building contracts, it also deals with trusts, consignment contracts and brokerage contracts. The building contracts dealt with under Contract Law include planning, inspection and building requirements for construction projects, and so are binding for architects and design engineers.

Land regulations

As has already been mentioned, China's socialist legal system is reflected above all in *land regulations*. The constitution lays down that there is no private land ownership in the cities; in the country and in suburban areas collective ownership of land that can be cultivated and hill land is still provided for, but there is no explicit private ownership of land. Rather than ownership rights, the state grants its citizens transferable *land utilization rights* (Article 10, Paragraph 4 of the constitution).

Rules about the transfer and encumbrances of land utilization rights are to be found in the relevant laws and regulations, especially the Land Administration Law (1998) and the Regulations on property development in the cities. With some significant exceptions, the land utilization rights are designed to be *similar to property*. They are subject to time limitations: for commercial and industrial use up to 40 or 50 years respectively, for residential use up to 70 years. There is a register in which all legal acts relating to a land utilization right have to be entered. For example, land utilization rights can also be mortgaged. In the case of disputes about the existence and scope of land utilization rights, local government administrative proceedings are slotted in before legal proceedings in the people's courts.

Land use planning

The Land Administration Law lays down a general *land use plan*. Here the law states that maintaining useful agricultural land, environmental protection and improved use of built-up land take precedence. The local and provincial governments have to keep to central government guidelines for their own planning, and to submit their plans to the higher authorities for approval.

As well as the general land use plans, there are the so-called *annual plans* for construction and for building project development and town planning. A system of statistical assessment and information processing is in place to oversee the implementation of agricultural, industrial and environmental guidelines. To guarantee better land exploitation, leaving land to lie fallow or derelict is punishable by fines and in severe cases by withdrawal of the right to use land.

If agricultural land is to be used as building land, central government permission is required above a certain size (25 or 70 hectares). This is intended to keep land use in check, or at least slow it down.

The Land Administration Law contains regulations about dispossession procedures and the compensation to be paid in such cases, land use fees and regulations relating to punishments and fines for violations of the law. It should be stressed that the law can declare dispossessions or land use permissions null and void if their scope and purposes are not compatible with the aims of the Land Administration Law.

The Law on Environmental Impact Assessment (2003) is particularly important for building projects. For projects that make a "considerable" impact on the environment it lays down a duty to draw up a comprehensive report on environmental effects and a permission procedure; registration alone is acceptable only for projects making "very little" impact on the environment.

Environmental impact assessment

In recent decades, China has set up a complex set of regulations for the treatment of foreign investment. The legal framework includes the laws on equity joint ventures, cooperative joint ventures and companies 100 per cent in foreign ownership among other things, along with their statutes of implementation, laws about foreign-owned holding companies and regulations about importing and exporting technology. This legislation is flanked by tax law regulations that grant advantages, some of them considerable, to Foreign Invested Enterprises (FIEs) in China.

Comprehensive regulations for foreign investments

From a legal point of view, the relationship of the special regulations applying to FIEs to civil legislation applicable to all companies in China is not always free of contradictions, and this can sometimes lead to considerable legal insecurity. The principal of treatment as nationals does apply, in other words FIEs, as Chinese companies, are to be subject to the legislation applying to all Chinese companies, but this principle is not applied with complete consistency.

Relationship of Foreign Investment Law to general legislation

B 2.2   Building and Planning Law

B 2.2.1   Principles of Chinese Building Law

The principal legal basis of the building sphere is the Contract Law (1999), which contains regulations on contracts for builders and architects, the Building Law (1998), the Administrative Regulations on Building Quality (2000, referred to as Quality Regulations below), the Tender Law (2000) and the Government Contract Law (2003).

An amendment to the Building Law has been in preparation for several years, and it was due to be passed in late 2006. Any fundamental changes this would make to the current law will be dealt with in the appropriate sections of this chapter.

Certificate of Competency system

Building companies cannot take part in projects just as they wish, but are granted Certificates of Competency relating to their qualifications and experience by the responsible authorities. These limit the admissible area of activity geographically, and in terms of the size of and demands made by the building project. Companies are reassessed annually, so a company can gradually increase its scope.

Separation of planning, erection and site supervision

Chinese Building Law distinguishes between planning, building and site supervision. For larger projects, building supervision has regularly to be handed over to a suitably qualified agency (which can also be a planning company), which should be independent of the other participants in the project. This separation is intended to guarantee the quality and safety of the project, though in the past it has been criticized by foreign companies as not in tune with international integrated project management (Engineering Procurement and Construction, EPC, turnkey). Site supervision, at least in cases of projects with state participation, remains separate from other building services in the Building Law Amendment as well, even though a tendency towards a more flexible approach can be detected here.

Contract by tender

The preferred mode for issuing building contracts is via public tender (Article 19 of the Building Law); building projects that are not suitable for open tender can be awarded directly. This ruling leaves scope for interpretation and abuse. So after the Building Law Amendment, direct contract award will be permissible only for projects that make particular demands in technological or specialist terms. The Amendment also forbids selecting companies while abusing administrative jurisdictions.

Planning and building permission

Once a project exceeds a certain size, planning and building permission must be granted before work starts. Building may not start without permission. The range of matters examined for permission of this kind is considerably wider than in the case of the German counterpart, for example. It looks not just at the precise elements in terms of Building and Planning Law, but also at features like financing the project, for example. After the amendment to the Building Law, full planning permission will be possible, but also individual permissions for certain sections and for certain building phases in terms of time. As well as the actual building and planning permission, the following must be available:

- permission to use the land
- planning permission from the local planning authorities

The planning permission procedure details vary from city to city and thus fall outside the useful scope of this book.

China has issued a large number of its own building and material standards. These often relate to Western standards (German standards DIN, for example), but they are not infrequently out of date. The material standards laid down by the State Economic and Trade Commission (SETC) are either advisory or mandatory.

Building and material standards

The mandatory standards must be observed by surveying and planning companies, and the planning requirements must meet these standards. Non-compliance with mandatory standards is punishable by fines. But planners are forbidden to specify manufacturers and sources for equipment and materials. One reason for these regulations, which are very rigid in part, is the Chinese legislators' justifiable concern that if mandatory regulations are not applied then inferior materials might be used, representing a threat to the safety of the building's users and the general public.

As a rule, only Chinese planning practices have precise knowledge of these standards. Many foreign planners see Chinese building and material standards as a major obstacle to entering the Chinese market. Chinese legislators have now acknowledged the fact that the standards do not reflect the current state of technology and to an extent tend to impede rather than promote building quality and safety: the Building Law Amendment prescribes immediate examination and amendment of a standard if it proves inappropriate for ensuring the quality of a building.

Familiarity with these standards

B 2.2.2   Foreign activity in the building trade

Foreigners have been involved in Chinese building projects since the start of Deng Xiaoping's openness policy in the early 1980s, though this was restricted to major projects at first, promoted by international institutions like the World Bank.

Foreign building firms came to China on a project-related basis in the 1980s and 1990s. To operate in China, foreign firms had to prove themselves capable of working on a particular project and were then granted a business licence – again project-related. Thus, at this time, longer presence in China could be restricted to founding a representative office, which was less laborious than setting up a subsidiary

Project-related participation system

company or joint venture. In the building sector, foreign participation was possible only in the following cases:

– projects financed exclusively with foreign capital
– projects financed by credits from international institutions, like the World Bank, for example, and where contracts were awarded on the basis of international tender
– Chinese-foreign joint venture projects that required technical expertise not available to the Chinese joint venture parties
– projects that were financed by the Chinese but which also required foreign expertise – here cooperation with Chinese partners was possible

Joint ventures in the building sector

From 1995, foreign firms were allowed to found joint ventures with Chinese partners in the building industry (with comparatively strict conditions in terms of minimum capital and participant qualification).

After 2004: a new regime for foreign activities in the building sector

The old project-related registration system ceased to apply when the regulations for administering foreign investment companies in the building industry (referred to as the Building Regulations) came into force on 1 April 2004. They were passed jointly by the Ministry of Construction and the Ministry of Foreign Trade. Now foreign companies who wish to take part in Chinese building projects have to set up a Foreign Investment Enterprise (known as a Building FIE). An exception is made for projects financed by international institutions like the World Bank or the Asian Development Bank (ADB). The advantages of the new ruling are:

– it is permissible for the first time to found 100 per cent subsidiaries of foreign firms in the building sector, though the scope of their activities is restricted
– 100 per cent subsidiary and building joint ventures are subject to the same qualification requirements as purely Chinese companies, and are thus treated as Chinese businesses
– 100 per cent subsidiaries may always take on building projects from FIEs not only in cases of emergency but at the request of the FIEs if the foreign joint venture partner is a majority partner in the FIE

The principal disadvantage of the new ruling is that foreign firms wishing to take on Chinese building projects are now compelled to have a permanent presence in China, requiring a considerable investment of work and capital. A further criticism is that foreign firms with an international reputation but without previous experience of

China receive only one certificate of competency at the lowest level for their 100 per cent subsidiary. Essentially this leaves three options for foreign newcomers:

- they work their way up the Chinese certificate of competency ladder over several years and gain access to more demanding projects in this way
- they find a Chinese partner for a joint venture who already has the desired certificate of competency
- the third variant means acquiring shares in an existing Chinese company. But it should be noted that the implementation clauses in the building regulations state that the *old* certificate of competency does not simply continue to be valid: a new assessment has to be made after shares have been acquired

However, it is not yet finally clear whether, in the case of a joint venture, the *most favoured* principle (namely, the highest available certificate of competency held by one of the partners applies to the whole joint venture) applies or whether the majority conditions in the joint venture do not in fact play a part in grading the qualification. Articles III.2.(2) and (3) of the Administrative Regulations seem to suggest a rather more restrictive tendency; certainly the building law amendment expressly admits differentiated recognition of member qualifications for tender or joint ventures.

B 2.2.3 The building contract

Regulations on building contracts are to be found in the Contract Law, in the Building Law and in the Building Quality Administrative Regulations. They are very sketchy.

Building contracts are to be concluded in writing. If this requirement is not met, the contract is null and void in the first place; but if one side has delivered and the other side accepted the service, the contract is valid nevertheless. *(Concluding contracts)*

Prime contracts in which the main contractor places survey and planning work with subcontractors are admissible, and so is the *separate placing* of surveying, planning and implementation work by the client with individual contractors who are then committed to the client directly. But the arbitrary splitting of a project intended to be treated as a whole into several separate individual projects is not admissible. *(Contract types)*

The building contract should contain clauses relating to the following points: *(Minimum contract content)*

- the scope of the project
- the building period

- a timetable for the individual trade branches
- quality
- cost
- delivery periods for technical equipment
- responsibility for delivering material and equipment
- payment
- acceptance
- quality guarantee and its validity period
- duties of the parties

Site supervision

As a rule the client will entrust site supervision to an appropriately qualified agency independent of others involved in the building process. The Building Law Amendment will relax this principle to the extent that separate site supervision will be required only for state-funded projects. The site supervision company employed represents the client to the building contractor. It is responsible for supervising the quality of the building work. If significant documents relating to the building work cannot be signed off by those responsible for site supervision, then the next building phase cannot proceed.

Inspection and supervision duties

Certain duties of supervision have to be borne in mind. The building contractor has duties of inspection and supervision in respect of the quality of the equipment and material delivered, and in particular the concrete delivered. The inspection must be documented in writing. If the building contractor discovers planning deficiencies in the course of building work, he is obliged to offer suggestions for rectification.

The contractor is further obliged to issue a declaration of guaranteed quality after the completed building has been accepted. This should precisely define the extent of the guarantee, its time limit and the contractor's obligations. Certain minimum guarantees for individual building components are laid down in the quality regulations.

Acceptance

Before the building is taken over acceptance is absolutely essential; without this, the building may not be taken over for use. The client should accept the building and provide a report for the responsible authorities; after inspecting this, the authorities can prevent the building from being taken over if need be and order a new acceptance procedure.

B 2.2.4   Liability

Liability to the client

The contractor is liable for deficiencies that can be ascribed to him in the prescribed quality features and is obliged to make them good free of charge or to rebuild. If this delays completion, he is liable for breach of contract, i.e. in principle he is obliged to pay compensation. In the case of quality deficiencies included in the aforementioned guarantee of quality, the contractor is obliged to repair and pay compensation. The contractual obligations come under the statute of limitations according to Article 135 of the General Principles of Civil Rights (GPC) after two years as a rule. However, this does not apply to claims covered by the quality guarantee; these should come under the statute of limitations within the scope of the guarantee agreement. At least the appropriate period of use for the building is considered agreed for foundations and load-bearing elements.

During the appropriate period of use for the building the contractor is liable to compensate third parties for detriment to persons and property. It is uncertain how the appropriate period of use can be more precisely defined. Agreements between the parties must ultimately influence determination of the appropriate period of use, as the aforementioned administrative regulations lay down that the contractor's contractual quality guarantee for foundations and load-bearing components should in any case cover at least their appropriate period of use, which emerges from the planning documents. The ruling in Article 137 of the GPC probably does represent a time limit: it states that all (indictable) claims come under the statute of limitations within 20 years of the breach of contract proceedings (for faulty planning or execution).

Third party liability

But it should be noted that the people's courts are authorized in exceptional cases to set a longer statute of limitations in terms of justice. Granting such exceptional status seems appropriate, particularly for large, important public buildings. There are indeed isolated voices in the Chinese specialist literature accepting continuance of liability for at least 25 years (in other words well beyond the regular limitation period laid down in the GPC).

To keep the liability risks under control, taking out appropriate insurance is urgently recommended.

If a main contractor passes individual jobs to subcontractors, the subcontractor is liable to the main contractor for the contractually defined quality of the work, and both are liable as joint guarantors to the client for the quality of this work.

Relationship between main and subcontractors

Though this is not expressly laid down in Contract Law, it is to be assumed that the few rules about the building contract are mandatory law, so consequently any contractual departure would be inadmissi-

Mandatory law

ble; but contractual definitions or specifications of vague, open legal terms must be admissible.

B 2.2.5   Architectural and engineering contracts

Chinese planning practices

Until a few years ago all the Chinese planning practices were in state hands, and many still are. As has already been mentioned, major weaknesses in Chinese architecture and engineering are lack of knowledge of modern, innovative building techniques, lack of knowledge of international building standards and general lack of experience in terms of international business, including the necessary linguistic knowledge. It is to be assumed that the discrepancies between the Chinese and leading international planning firms will be reduced in the years to come, not least because of cooperation between Chinese and foreign architects and engineers.

Classifying planning practices

Chinese planning practices are divided into four classes: A, B, C and D. Class A planning practices are not subject to any restrictions regarding the scale, difficulty or location of an advertised project. Classes B and C are restricted by the relevant province of origin or the planning practice's location, and class D is not allowed to plan any underground structures.

Cooperation between Chinese and foreign planners

In principle there are three paths open to foreign companies wishing to work in China in the planning and engineering fields:

- setting up a foreign-invested planning enterprise (joint venture or 100 per cent subsidiary) or buying a stake in an existing Chinese compan;
- setting up an FIE restricted to consultancy services
- providing cross-border planning services for or with a Chinese planning practice

Planning enterprises with foreign participation

The regulations on the administration of foreign-invested companies for building and technical planning (henceforth called planning regulations) are extremely important for foreign planners and engineers working in China. They came into effect in 2002. The planning regulations are structured like the aforementioned building regulations. But they differ significantly from the building regulations in that foreign planning firms (Foreign-Investment Design Enterprises, FIDE) are subject to stricter rules under the procedure for issuing a certificate of competency than Chinese planners. Just like Chinese planners, they go through the assessment procedure described above (Articles 11, 15 of the planning regulations). This means that their lack of experience with Chinese building projects – even if all the rest of their qualifications are outstanding – places them in the lowest class. In addition, the planning regulations impose other burdens on the FIDE:

- 25 per cent of the staff of a 100 per cent subsidiary required according to the certificate of competency must be foreign architects or engineers who are registered in China; for joint ventures the figure is one eighth
- each FIDE foreign expert registered in China is obliged to be present in China for at least six months (with consequences relating to taxation)

These rules erect considerable barriers against foreign firms who wish to become extensively involved in the planning sphere, and consequently they have been violently criticized by foreign companies and organizations. They cannot survive for long under the WTO regime. Apart from setting up a new FIDE – alone or in the form of a joint venture with a Chinese partner – the same question naturally arises as for building projects: is it possible to set up an FIDE by acquiring a stake in an existing Chinese planning practice? This should definitely be treated positively. We feel that in a case like this the stricter planning regulation rules do not apply in respect of the staffing ratio, the obligation to be present, etc.; however, it is to be anticipated that the certificate of competency will have to be reassessed.

The provincial governments are responsible for issuing certificates of competency, but issuing a class A certificate of competency for the building field needs approval from the State Council.

Foreign architects and engineers, as well as being able to set up a planning practice in the form of an FIE in China, also have the option of offering consultancy services, likewise in the form of an FIE. The prevailing opinion is that this is not covered by the tight establishment and activity requirements of the planning regulations. But this does not mean that the foreign founder's qualifications are not checked by the responsible authorities; here, however, the authorities have wider scope for discretion, with all the attendant advantages and disadvantages for the applicant. The advantage of such an arrangement are obvious:

Consultancy services in China

- lower capital and staff commitments than when setting up a planning FIE
- hence greater flexibility and – given increasingly intense competition – cost advantages
- more complex tasks can be dealt with by working with Chinese partners on specific cases

The essential disadvantage of such an approach is exclusion from many tenders through lack of a competency certificate for certain planning services.

Cross-border coopera-
tion possibilities Other forms of cooperation between Chinese and foreign planning practices are possible alongside the joint venture foundations provided for in the planning regulations and purchasing a stake in an existing Chinese planning practice, which also results in a joint venture. Relevant in practice is, above all, cooperation in specific cases between Chinese and foreign planning practices that have not set up an FIDE in China. This sphere is now also regulated under the provisional rules for building planning in China by foreign enterprises (2004, henceforth called the Provisional Rules). Key elements of these rules are:

- duty of inspection and signature by Chinese planners (architects, engineers)
- cross-border payments (in currency) is admissible in principle
- minimum content of cooperation contracts, which should define respective spheres of responsibility
- obligation on the client to demand production of the (foreign) certificates of competency and other documents from foreign companies

Internationally accepted specimen contracts

The principal specimen contracts to be accepted internationally are those published by the Fédération Internationale des Ingenieurs-Conseils (FIDIC), which is based in Geneva. As well as this, there is whole range of specimen building contracts originating mainly from Anglo-Saxon law (England and the USA). The Orgalime Turnkey Contracts for Industrial Works should also be mentioned in this context. They are published by the Organization for Liaison of European Metal Industries and intended for use in turnkey provision of industrial complexes. Because the FIDIC contracts are so outstandingly important, and also making their presence felt in China, their key concepts are laid out below. All these sets of rules are directed at engineers.

FIDIC Red Book The *FIDIC Red Book* lays down the legal relationship between client, contractor and planner. Essentially it follows the construction contract model, i.e. the client employs the building contractor or planner directly. Remuneration is calculated on the basis of a system of unit prices and quantities. Another special feature is the emphasis placed on the planner or engineer, who can function as a referee between contractor and client in case of dispute, for example. However, the *Red Book* does not rule on legal relations between client and planner.

The *FIDIC Silver Book* is applied mainly to build-operate-transfer projects, i.e. to buildings constructed for turnkey handover built by the contractor, who is also responsible for planning, for an inclusive price. The contractor is subject to greater risks than under the *Red Book*. The *Silver Book* provides rules for the classic turnkey building: there is a design, which has to be made more precise in planning terms (e.g. statics, working plans) and then realized.

FIDIC Silver Book

The *FIDIC Yellow Book* takes another step forward and includes all the design planning as well. It implements the plant (design-and-build) contract concept: the contractor takes on planning and realization for an inclusive price paid on account according to the progress of the building work (instalment payments laid down in a payment plan). This contract is often used for building power stations and plants.

FIDIC Yellow Book

In China, contracts have been based on the FIDIC rules largely for major projects involving international participation and finance. The World Bank and the Asian Development Bank in particular regularly insist on the FIDIC rules (especially the *Red Book*). The FIDIC rules have so far been used only rarely for medium-sized projects. In practice this means that, for large projects at least, it is possible to rely on the basic framework and terminology of the FIDIC's *General Conditions*, but drawing up the special conditions is then left for the individual case.

Applying the FIDIC rules in China

As these contracts cover planning services and are widely used internationally, planners (architects and engineers) are often brought in by building firms and, as a rule, work as subsequent contractors for the building firm abroad.

Legal requirements for architects' and engineers' contracts

Provisions for architects' or planners' contracts are even more sparse than those for building contracts in general. What is laid down is the minimum content for the architect's contract, which should cover the following contractual conditions:

- a time limit for providing the relevant planning information and documents
- a budget estimate

– establishment of quality requirements
– fee provisions
– and also other conditions for cooperation, such as dispute resolution procedures, for example

If delay or error on the part of the architect or engineer delays the construction process, that party is obliged to repair and take a reduction in his fee, and to pay compensation. Conversely, the architect can require payment for additional expenditure brought about through faults on the client's side (Article 285, Contract Law).

Building Law Amendment: payment provisions

In practice, securing payment for those involved in building continues to be a serious problem. This is why the Building Law Amendment contains some important provisions about the client's payment obligations to his fellow parties to the contract, especially to the planners. These are that the contract should fix a payment method with the planners. Agreed advance payments for contractors and planners is a possibility, and so are payment according to building progress or agreeing an inclusive price.

The contractor or planner should submit a final invoice after completion and acceptance. If the parties cannot agree on how high this should be, the contractor or planner can commission an expert to examine and fix the fee; this expert's decisions are binding on the client. If he falls behind with payments, the planner has the right to withhold his services, and also the right to demand interest on delayed payments and compensation from other losses suffered through delay.

Liability

In the first place, the architect or planner registered in China who signed the planning documents is liable for planning (Article 19, Clause 2 of the Building Quality Regulations). The position, in principle, is this: architects or engineers are liable to their immediate contract partner, in other words either the main contractor or the client, for mistakes they have made. If the architect or engineer is engaged as a subcontractor, the contractor and the architect are liable to the client as joint debtors (Article 29, Paragraph 2 of the Building Law).

Liability to third parties

The provision in Article 282 of the Contract Law that the contractor is liable for physical injuries or loss of property incurred during the appropriate time for use of the building and which can be attributed to the contractor must also be applicable to the planner to the extent that detriment to body or property can be attributed to his planning. At least, the planner must expect recourse from the contractor if this is claimed by damaged third parties. The planner must also include difficulties in determining the appropriate period of use in his calculations and provide appropriate insurance cover where necessary.

As a rule, planning work is kept separate from site supervision in China. Hence architects and engineers are generally only subject to liability for faulty planning (design and build projects come under different rules). This liability applies to foreign partners involved in cross-border cooperation without an FIE only to a limited extent, as the Chinese planning partner is contractually bound to inspect and sign off the foreign partner's planning documents. If the foreign partner is (jointly) responsible for the planning error but is not the client's direct contract partner, at best recourse by the Chinese planning practice against the foreign planner can be considered. If an FIDE commits planning errors resulting in loss or damage, then it is responsible in principle itself.

Planning errors

If a planner interrupts the building process through delay or inadequate planning he is contractually obliged to repair, to reduce his fee and to pay compensation (Article 280, Contract Law).

Extent of liability

There is no legislation for cases where a building is completed on time, but after completion it emerges that the planner did not meet the contractual requirements. Here a distinction needs to be made: if the planner has made a contractual guarantee, then there is no question about his liability. The legal situation may be different if no such explicit guarantee has been given. It must be assumed that compensation is also to be paid in principle in such cases, though it must be open to proof, and measurable (for example, in the case of under-provision in relation to floor area figures). If the contrary is the case, a penal sum has to be fixed contractually.

Fees

In principle China's Price Law also applies to services provided by architects and engineers, but it does allow the responsible authorities to lay down prices for individual services of particular significance to the public good – and this also includes planning services. Accordingly, in 2002 the State Council and the Ministry of Construction jointly issued administrative regulations for the fees of surveyors and planners in the building industry and based on this the standards for building planners' fees. Essentially they say this:

Price law

- the state lays down recommended prices for building projects in-volving over 5 million Rmb (= just under 500,000 euros); pricing is left to the parties involved for projects below this threshold
- there is a basic fee for design and implementation planning; addi-tional payment can then be required for additional services
- the recommended price can be exceeded by up to 25 per cent for projects of outstanding quality (for example, those using new technologies or that are especially environmentally friendly)

It is uncertain whether the price regulations are also binding on foreign architects working in China. The wording suggests that the regulations apply to all building projects inside China. And yet the relevant clauses say that foreign architects can at least cite exemp-tions if their fees deviate from the said regulations.

So a foreign planner's fee, insofar as the technological demands of a project require his participation, should be negotiated by the parties on the basis of the price codes; in other words, the fee regu-lations are simply a non-binding frame of reference here. This derives from Article 12 of the above-mentioned provisional rules, according to which Chinese fee-setting standards apply on the one hand, but, on the other, payment is to be fixed by negotiations taking account of international practice and the actual volume of work.

In practice, architects' fees turn out to be considerably lower than in the West: unofficial figures usually suggest 50 per cent, occasionally also between 20 and 30 per cent. This is due, above all, to fierce competition and to the fact that the country is still comparatively underdeveloped.

Currency regime

If planning services are provided by a planning FIE or officially by a Chinese planning practice in China, these are to be paid for in the Chinese currency renminbi (Rmb). Payment in foreign currency is not permitted. However, such sums are convertible through au-thorized banks, though only against correct documentation (proof of origin for the sums involved, proof of tax paid, proof of a decision on profit-sharing by the FIE). If services are provided across borders – for example by foreign planning offices directly for large Chinese planning offices or FIEs authorized for foreign trade – payment in foreign currency (dollars, euros) can be considered.

B 2.2.6 Contract drafting
Even though it is beyond the scope of this book to cover contract drafting in full, the most important aspects will be dealt with below.

For international contracts, the parties have an option in principle to agree to apply the law of the land of origin of one of the parties (or even that of a third country). In China the following should be taken into account here: it is not possible to choose a foreign legal system as the basis for contracts between two Chinese parties – and FIEs count as such. However, it is possible in principle to consider choosing a legal system for cross-border services, as for example in the case of contracts between a foreign planner and a Chinese partner. The problem here is that Chinese courts not infrequently ignore a choice of legal system. Chinese legislation is interpreted as binding (*ordre public*).

Choice of legal system

Chinese Price Law for architects and engineers (see above) is to be seen as binding in principle, but leaves a great deal of room for manoeuvre in the case of advanced projects.

The scope of services is not derived from fee structures or the requirements of an association, as in some European countries, but has to be agreed in detail. To avoid subsequent disputes about requests for changes, special services and the like, the services agreed should be defined as precisely and in as much detail as possible.

Scope of services

One of the biggest problems foreign planners face in China is securing payment. There are various ways of achieving this.

Payment

Some planners insist on advances of up to 50 per cent of the sum contracted from their Chinese clients. This requires an appropriate negotiating position, but is quite usual in China.

But payment at fixed times (monthly, quarterly), however advantageous it may be for the planner, is not customary in China, and is likely to be difficult to negotiate as a rule.

The method that seems easiest to make work in practice is to secure payment using a system based on fixed building phases. The bill of quantity concept laid down in the FIDIC rules and explained below has already been applied in China: an acceptable rule of thumb is that not more than 30 days of work will be done in advance without payment. A further basic rule is that the lion's share of the work should not be done before a significant proportion of the fee has been paid.

Care is needed when using fit for purpose clauses. An Anglo-American legal viewpoint accepts that the contractor (subcontractor, planner) accepts liability for achieving planning aims independently of negligence. Such clauses are not expressly applied in the FIDIC rules, but required in part.

Liability rules in the contract

To summarize, as discussed above, these legal rulings on the planner's liability for third-party detriment to persons or property through deficiencies in the construction work that can be attributed to the planner's actions are binding and cannot be effectively modified by shifting costs to third parties (for example the future user of the building). Even choice of a legal system is likely to be ineffective here – at least in the eyes of a Chinese court – as it excludes the claims of such injured parties.

Minimizing contractual liability

There are various ways of minimizing personal liability:

- minimizing liability by demarcating areas of responsibility: it seems sensible, especially with reference to any Chinese partner practice there may be, to fix each partner's areas of responsibility as precisely as possible

- claims for exemption against contract partners (main contractors): here for example an exemption clause against the partner covering claims by third parties could be built in

- liability to the customer/main contractor: the above recommendations apply in general in terms of claims from the client or main contractor arising from detriment caused by planning errors. It is recommended that appropriate periods of limitation be fixed for compensation claims by the client or main contractor

- minimizing liability by setting up an FIDE. One key advantage of setting up an FIDE is minimizing liability risks by interposing an independent legal entity in the form of an FIDE. Of course, this kind of risk minimization can also be achieved offshore through the participation of a subsidiary based in a third country

Contract penalties

Contract penalties are admissible in principle in Chinese law and also to be recommended, but there is still a possibility for those affected to adapt contract penalties to the detriment actually suffered through the people's courts. This option cannot be modified contractually (except by a choice of legal system, see above).

Notifying defects

Defects or complaints should be notified formally to avoid future dispute. This also includes setting deadlines for the notification of defects.

Settling disputes

It is essential to regulate dispute settlement procedures contractually. Here it makes sense to agree on an arbitration body to take an interim decision that can be examined by a court or court of arbitration if the need arises. This is also favoured by the FIDIC rules. As well as this, because of the imponderability of Chinese justice, it is advisable as a rule – except for smaller projects – to choose an arbitration court. This will be dealt with in greater detail in the next chapter.

B 2.2.7 Implementing the law

Implementing demands by foreign creditors against Chinese companies is regularly made more difficult by the following circumstances:

Implementing demands by foreign creditors

- the phenomenon of local protectionism
- the problem of a lack of professionalism and reliability in Chinese justice
- the disappearance of the contract partner
- the fact that foreign legal decisions cannot be enforced

It is a frequent occurrence for partners to "go underground", abandoning their place of business and their company and either disappearing from the scene completely or – armed with a new company and a new address – starting to trade again a short time later and not feeling responsible for demands made by their former partner. Such practices, which are also disapproved of in principle in Chinese law, are extremely difficult to get to grips with by legal means without a great deal of effort and expense. When working with state planning offices there is also a danger that these will be abolished and the former employees will set up private planning practices without accepting the former legal entity's obligations.

The possibility should also be mentioned that the parties – perhaps at the insistence of the foreign partner – may have agreed on a foreign legal domicile. The greatest care is needed here, as judgments by German courts, for example, are regularly not recognized in China, and thus cannot be enforced.

If the parties have agreed on a Chinese legal domicile, the Chinese creditor has a certain home advantage at first. But he can only make use of this if the foreign contract partner has significant assets in China that can be seized to enforce any decision (an FIE's assets, for example). Enforcing judgments by Chinese courts abroad meets with the same difficulties as in the converse case.

Implementing demands by Chinese creditors

It is not possible to make a general recommendation about clauses relating to legal domicile and arbitration. The advantages of an arbitration court are greater expertise and the fact that a legally binding title is acquired more quickly, but there is a disadvantage in the costs, which are considerably higher in some respects. Foreign

Clauses relating to legal domicile and arbitration

planners must be very careful to ensure that their liability insurance covers the choice of an arbitration court: this is not the case for standard contracts in Germany, for example.

For large projects, it is preferable to choose an arbitration court from the circle of well-known international institutions, like the Stockholm Chamber of Commerce or the Handelskammer in Zurich, for example. Decisions by "ad hoc arbitration courts", in other words courts constituted especially for the case that is to be decided, are not recognized in China. It is also possible to choose a domestic Chinese arbitration court, like the CIETAC (China International Economic and Trade Arbitration Commission) in Beijing, for example, whose list of judges also includes foreigners. This can have certain advantages in terms of enforcement in certain circumstances, as arbitration verdicts by CIETAC are not tainted by the "foreigner handicap".

For the reasons mentioned above, agreeing on a foreign legal domicile is not advisable as a rule. Inside China it makes sense to choose a court in one of the big cities, preferably from a city that is not home to the Chinese partner's company headquarters.

B 2.3   Invitations to tender

A few years ago now – at about the same time as a parallel development in the European Union – the Chinese government recognized that a transparent set of rules was needed for awarding public contracts. As in Europe, the Chinese also came to the conclusion that contract award by public tender offered an approach that, as a rule, leads to the best and cheapest solutions and at the same time helps to check corruption, which is widespread in China. So China imposed a fixed set of rules on the public contract award sphere – comparable with the wide-ranging area to which the EU contract award directives apply – in the form of the Tendering Act (1999) the Government Contract Award Act (2002) and a large number of subsidiary regulations.

A large volume of public commissions falls under China's tendering regime: semi-official estimates work on an annual contract sum of up to 4,000 billion Rmb (approx. 400 billion euros) by the year 2008. So it is worth addressing China's Contract Award Law.

Legal bases

Chinese Contract Award Law is determined by a hierarchy of standards that can be broken down into four levels:

- on the top level are the above-mentioned Tendering Act and the Government Contract Award Act

- on the second level, decrees by the State Council have to be taken into account
- on the third level there are regulations relating to implementation and administration passed by the State Development Planning Commission, SDPC, or other authorities (especially the specialist ministries or provincial authorities)
- on the lowest level, administration orders on administering and supervising projects have to be taken into account

As well as this there are local regulations that are not always in harmony with the national rules. The most important local complex of rules that should be mentioned are the Beijing tendering regulations, which stand alongside the national standards as the basis tendering procedures for construction and infrastructure projects for the 2008 Olympic Games in Beijing.

The Tendering Act is restricted in its application to major projects in the infrastructure sphere, financed either through international credits or from fixed capital funds, while the Government Contract Award Act extends the scope of application of the tendering regulations to all forms of state contract award. This affects contract awards for building projects and for services, and the acquisition of goods above certain threshold values, which are summed up in a central government contract award catalogue. Military procurement is explicitly excluded from the area of application of the Government Contract Award Act, and contract award by nationalized companies is excluded implicitly. The Government Contract Award Act contains detailed regulations on tendering procedures, which are not included in the Tendering Act. The Government Contract Award Act also lays down those exceptional cases for which tendering is not needed.

Relationship between the Government Contract Award Act and the Tendering Act

The Government Contract Award Act lays down that domestic tenders are to be preferred in principle unless it is impossible or not commercially viable to award to a domestic bidder, or procurement is being made for use outside China. This is a regrettable, retrograde legislative step that has been frequently criticized. Clarification is needed in this respect about the extent to which planning FIEs enjoy domestic status. In the author's opinion this should be affirmed unreservedly; but it is to be feared that in practice the authorities (as has happened in other contexts) will also take the majority circumstances into account.

Favouring domestic bidders

Chinese contract award law acknowledges two tendering procedures, public and non-public contract award. Non-public award means an

Kinds of tender

invitation to tender issued to a closed circle of bidders. In practice, especially when large building projects are being put out to tender (the Beijing underground, for example), a pre-qualification procedure is often carried out. Here a public request for tenders is made in the first place. For this tender, reference is made to a system of generalized qualification criteria that the interested companies have to satisfy. Paragraph 18 of the Tendering Act does not specify whether the bidders qualify in a first stage or as part of the overall assessment of the tender. The ruling laid down in Paragraph 16 of the Beijing tendering rules provides for a two-stage pre-qualification procedure, but leaves it to the client to fix the pre-qualification criteria. Here a certain state qualification certificate for projects of a certain size in a certain segment of the construction and infrastructure sector has to be submitted (the leading engineer, for example, must show a class A certificate for engineering and bridge construction form the People's Republic of China's Ministry of Construction).

The Tendering Act leaves it for the province to specify the cases for which a public or a non-public tender has to take place. So the Beijing tendering regulations make public tendering the rule. Non-public tendering is admissible only if only a very small circle of potential bidders can be considered anyway because of special technological or environmental requirements (Paragraph 11, nos. 1–3 of the Beijing tendering conditions).

General avoidance ban

All state offices are obliged to put work out to tender whenever this is legally prescribed; there is a general ban on avoiding the tendering laws.

Ban on discriminatory treatment

Contract Award Law insists on open and fair tendering procedures and forbids discriminatory treatment of individual bidders. Unlawful agreements between bidders and between individual bidders and the client are also forbidden, and punishable under certain circumstances.

Team bids / consortia

Contract Award Law permits team bids. Each member of the bidding team must meet the qualifications laid down in the invitation to tender individually; a team bid will be categorized according the qualifications of its least qualified member, which does not exactly make team bids more attractive to highly qualified companies. Agreements between bidding teams that would restrict competition are inadmissible; equally inadmissible is pressure from the party inviting to tender to form a bidding team with the intention of restricting competition (Paragraph 32 of the Tendering Act).

The party inviting to tender can carry out the invitation to tender itself, or can appoint a so-called tendering agent. Tendering agents are companies approved by the Chinese state specializing in such procedures.

Tendering agents

A period of at least two weeks must elapse between announcing the invitation to tender in publications available nationwide and the end of the tender period. Bids that are submitted late are not considered. Bids are opened in the presence of all bidders. An assessment commission then evaluates the bids. This commission is made up of a group of experts assembled either by the client or a tendering agent. Persons interested in the outcome of the tendering process are to be excluded from the assessment commission. The assessment commission chooses the bid to be accepted; the selection criteria are kept strictly secret. The assessment commission's recommendation is binding on the client. The successful bidder and the client should conclude a written contract within 30 days of the award.

Order of procedure

The company winning the award may not hand the commission over to third parties for implementation, either in whole or in substantial parts. However, it is admissible to employ subcontractors for non-substantial parts of the commission.

Subcontractors

Violations of the above-mentioned rules of procedure are punishable by fine. Penal sanctions also apply in cases of fraudulent co-operation to the disadvantage of the state between several bidders or between bidders and client. Even more important for the disadvantaged bidders are the regularly occurring legal consequences the award being declared null and void. If a state institution does not put a project out to tender even though it should have done so, measures that can be taken include freezing the funds set aside for the project temporarily, or stopping the project itself for the time being. In the case of particularly serious violations against contract award law, disadvantaged bidders may have recourse to a compensation claim. This could happen, for example, in the case of collusive co-operation between several bidders or between one bidder and the client, if the client or members of the assessment commission are being bribed in an attempt to secure the award.

Legal consequences of violations

If the Tender Award Laws are violated, bidders have the right to make a counter-representation to the client within a certain period or to appeal against the board of control responsible. If these come to nothing, an action can be filed in the people's courts.

Legal remedies

Internationally financed
tender invitations

Both the Tendering Act and the Government Contract Award Act allow deviations from the act's rules for tender invitations with international finance or financial aid, provided that this does not run counter to the public welfare interests of the People's Republic of China.

Invitations to tender for
construction planning

The most important feature here is that changes to the invitation to tender conditions are admissible only if they are announced to all bidders at the latest 15 days before the tender period expires. The period between the announcement and the submission of tenders, the tender period, should be at least 30 days, in the case of top-priority projects 45 days. It is 20 days for invitations to tender for rough draft planning.

Foreign planners taking part in domestic tender bids need permission to do so at provincial level. As the design to be submitted also has to be signed off and stamped by a planning practice authorized to sign, it is practically out of the question for foreign planners to take part in Chinese planning competitions without Chinese partners or their own planning FIE.

It is also worth mentioning that the above-mentioned rules also apply to large projects at central level and to internationally financed projects.

Award practice

In practice it can be assumed that the above-mentioned rules for awarding contracts will be complied with for large projects on the central plane, and for projects financed internationally. World Bank projects or those (co-)financed by the Asia Development Bank anyway have to comply with specific standards expressly admitted by Chinese Contract Award Law.

Violations of contract award law occur constantly below this level. The following should be mentioned in particular:

– no invitation to tender for projects that actually must be put out to tender; shortening the arranged tender periods to the disadvantage of non-local bidders or announcing invitations to tender in comparatively unknown trade publications rather than in internationally regarded media available all over the country should also be seen in the context
– collusive cooperation between individual bidders and the client
– non-responsible authorities interfering in the tender procedure, not infrequently with the intention of gaining preference for domestic bidders (called "local protectionism")
– bribing members of the assessment commission or of the client's employees responsible for the award

This list is not definitive. Foreign planners should take particular care to ensure that they have the necessary domestic proofs of qualification either themselves (as a planning FIE) or in the person of their Chinese partner. As well as this, they should establish the cost of their participation in the competition contractually in advance, and secure that the copyright of their designs is protected through contractual and other measures.

B 2.4 Copyright protection for architects and engineers

The Chinese Copyright Protection Act (2002) recognizes buildings as also copyrightable in Article 4, Paragraph 9. The regulations for implementing the Copyright Protection Act define this more precisely to the effect that buildings are to be copyrightable to the extent that they carry aesthetic significance in the form of the building or its components. So the building must represent a creative achievement. Plans, designs, and drawings relating to its construction are protected with the building.

Fundamentals of copyright protection

As in the field of intangible rights protection in general in China, considerable deficiencies can be identified in implementing the intellectual property rights of architects and engineers in practice. Imitations of design proposals by competitors in architectural competitions, for example, have occurred, and identical versions of buildings in a particular location have been erected without permission in a different city or province. This is due partly to defects in Chinese justice as a whole, and also to the fact that the idea of a building as a work protected by copyright has not yet been generally acknowledged in China.

Legal practice

An additional factor is that the relevant literature and practice has not yet interpreted the term "work" definitively, and there is continuing argument in particular about the term "creative level", which derives from German law (*Schöpfungshöhe*), as a requirement for copyright protection. Disputes about copyright protection are already pending before German courts, but at the time of writing there have been no judgments by the Supreme Court.

About the author:
Dr Christian Gloyer is a lawyer specializing in direct foreign investment in China; he has a command of spoken and written Mandarin. He worked first of all for a large German practice in Munich and Hong Kong, and then as a freelance lawyer in Berlin. He founded the Society of BGKW Lawyers in 2004. The society serves both German businesses with commitments in China and also Chinese businesses operating in Germany.

Planning in China

C 1   Breaking into the market and procurement

Werner Sübai

I was invited to China in the year 2001 because I got in touch with a Chinese developer I had met on my first trip to China. The Chinese client showed us a variety of projects that were about to be developed, which led to the first project-related contact. After I had come back to Germany a lot of time was spent discussing the project and the general conditions attached to it, but we didn't receive a planning commission, and development of the project ground to a halt on the data highway from Shanghai to Düsseldorf because of the geographical distance and the resulting communication difficulties.

HPP's first realistic opportunity to break into the Chinese market came with an invitation to enter a housing construction competition in Shanghai. Different residential construction types were to be developed for a new satellite town, and there was even a modest fee for the work. HPP won the competition in spring 2003 and worked on the project to the permission planning stage. The first project provided a platform for further activity in China: from this point, we were very busy on the Chinese planning scene. We took part in competitions and studies, and devised selected planning concepts at clients' requests. The exotic nature of the work and the interest generated by something new have long since moved into the background, subsumed under everyday architectural routine.

Contacts and access opportunities can arise quite individually, as in our case, but parallels and generally valid systems can be identified, and these will be dealt with in the chapter that follows.

Breaking into the Chinese market

The most important factor for breaking into the Chinese market is how well the architecture practice is known (internationally). A high profile gives architects an entrée with clients who are interested in Western planning quality. As a rule, the Chinese are convinced that the extent to which a practice is known and, above all, the number of people it employs give a clear indication of the quality and professional standard of the planning offered.

How well known are you?

Ill. 1.1: HHP designed four different housing types for Anting New Town, a "satellite" development in south-west Shanghai: multi-storey apartments on the block
periphery, . . .

Ill. 1.2: . . . town houses, . . .

Regular publications contribute to conveying the extent to which
an architecture practice is known and the number of projects it has
planned and realized. Print is rated very highly as a medium in
China.

Ill. 1.3: ... point buildings and ...

Ill. 1.4: ... a long building.

Another essential is an internationally slanted website. The Internet represents a first contact possibility and a source of information for a Chinese client looking for a suitable overseas architect. It is an advantage if both publications and the practice's own website are constructed in English and, ideally, in Mandarin (the same applies to the print media, of course).

Hence articles in Chinese magazines and architecture-related Chinese Internet forums are another building block for targeted marketing.

Presentations and introductions

Once contact has been made with Chinese clients, a small account of current projects in a handy flyer supports personal procurement on the spot. This flyer is essentially to be seen as a business card for your own practice, referring to the interactive practice presentation as a fundamental procurement tool. Such presentations are an ideal way of putting forward the practice's individual qualities and possible specialisms, or even projects in additional detail. The Chinese – unlike the Europeans – are besotted with technology, and regrettably also very demanding. For this reason, every form of presentation and project introduction should be designed more elaborately than is customary in Europe. Chinese clients like to see pictures. The person who shows the most impressive pictures must also be the best planner, or at least that is how many clients see it.

Making contact

There are various ways for foreign architecture practices to make contact with potential Chinese clients: via competitions, direct contacts, networking, business trips and trade fairs, and a great deal more. It is important not to work on the basis of achieving success in the short term. If a European architecture practice becomes involved in the Chinese market, the project should be handled by a person who would like to be committed personally and professionally for the medium or long term (proprietor, director, partner). Relationships can only be built up via individuals who are constantly present, and that individual's position in the office hierarchy is more important to Chinese clients than is the case in Europe. If the contact person is a director or practice proprietor, then it is assumed that the practice is genuinely and keenly interested, but if employees are dispatched as project leaders, this can be interpreted as lack of interest.

As a rule, it is possible to solve the great mentality and language problem only via Chinese architects who either work in the German practice or are employed in its Chinese branch. A foreign architect who speaks Mandarin and is thus in a position to communicate in China without an intermediary does not need a Chinese representative to the same extent. But it is essential that this architect, too, has local expertise at his disposal, so that he can understand and use structures and connections.

Competitions as a procurement method

Competitions are an important procurement method in China. An architecture practice needs to have a few sets of events with a positive

Ill. 1.5: The new Landmark Building for the Nanjing International Financial Mansion Center: the entire complex and the 330 metre high skyscraper are based on a characteristically innovative and sustainable concept.

outcome under its belt before it can expect to be invited to take part in a competition. The practice has to do something itself to bring the first invitations in: visit city authorities, put itself forward, write to potential clients and convince them of its abilities. This is best done personally and on the spot. Direct contact with the client in the early phases of the project helps to gain acceptance and understanding of the practice's particular approach to design. Working as a result of the competition then produces a network of connections through which the practice can gradually develop.

Ill. 1.6: The Fenglin Biomedical Center in Shanghai's historic Xuhui quarter: the urban concept for the campus points to the future by combining Knowledge Hub requirements with the interests of sustainable urban reconstruction.

Local presence

Branches as a procurement base

HPP is working on setting up a base in China, by making regular trips there. A local office is a key procurement tool: you are readily accessible to the Chinese client, have an infrastructure in place on the spot and can act effectively without wasting any time.

Here it is important not to forget how big China is: China's north–south axis is as long as the distance from Norway to Sicily. This market is not comparable with the European market, and you do yourself a great favour by restricting the radius of your campaign.

Dealing with differences of mentality

Making a deliberate effort to address differences in mentality between Europeans and Chinese people makes mutual understanding easier. Such differences can vary considerably within China itself. The biggest difference between procurement at home and in China is that, as a rule, it is not possible to communicate directly. Very few potential Chinese clients speak English or German, so that, as a rule, communication has to be via a third party. When presenting a practice's work you thus have to rely entirely on design and technical quality, which are conveyed through publications, presentations and flyers, and through the abilities of the interpreter and your own Chinese colleagues. It is also difficult for outsiders to find out which employee of a Chinese company is the right contact for his particular field, or who is responsible for internal decision-making processes. It is not the same as America and Europe, where hierarchies and responsibilities are open, and generally known, you have to find out about them gradually. Often decisions are not made in the circle in which they are discussed, but without the architect in a higher-ranking group.

Communication processes and discussions also proceed differently from our familiar practice. We can usually reach an understanding about a particular planning topic rapidly and pertinently in Germany or Europe, even in a circle of people who are meeting for the first time. Here we attach great importance to clearing up problems and agreeing who, among those present, can contribute something to solving a specific problem. Discussions of this kind are usually not hierarchical here, but open to anyone who can contribute to the matter in hand. We work within defined project structures aiming to realize a building project that has previously been fixed in terms of content, design and quality, within a certain time and cost framework. We define the aims as precisely as possible before we embark on the project.

German or European communication processes

In China it often seems to work exactly the other way round: the client sets off with a particular idea without knowing exactly what his target looks like or how he is going to reach it. The planning, or rather the aim of the planning, is not precisely defined, and thus open to a range of influences for change. It can happen that no one has researched whether there was a need or a market for the new building before planning started, and so the design has to be adapted to deal with completely new requirements, locations, volumes and functions during the planning process. It is also possible that the Chinese client might develop certain formal ideas that cannot be accommodated structurally. These or similar situations occur all the time, and as a planner you have to find the necessary flexibility to handle them.

Chinese communication

Eating together to ensure mutual esteem is a ritual that corresponds in significance to our project progress plan. Often important information is mentioned informally on the side. China is still a newly industrialized country, and the Chinese are fond of showing off their technical achievements and the prosperity associated with them. They also expect to be "courted" by the guests in the same way. A little present from your home town, something typical of the area, shows where you come from and helps to break the ice when getting to know people.

Procurement investment levels

Payment for competitions

Reports and competitions are very demanding in terms of presentation time and effort, but a fee is usually paid for them. And prize money is often paid to competition prizewinners, in addition to the fee. Payment levels for reports and competitions depend on the project aims and the status of the planning job; costs will often not be covered. Additionally, the brief is often changed during the competition process. But, as a rule, there is no possibility of adjusting the fee to match the actual time and money spent on the project.

As the fee is usually paid in arrears and suing for fees or even copyright is seldom likely to be successful, it is advisable to assess how serious the client is, in order to form an impression about the likelihood of working with him against the background of the amount of work needed. Here you either use your own representatives and contacts or take advice from local business consultancies, like the SHK/GCIC (German Chamber of Foreign Trade) or other independent institutions.

Maintaining and developing contacts

In general, procurement in the international context demands more time and expense than in one's own country. Long journeys, jet lag and the strange surroundings add further pressure, and lead to extraordinary stress for the people involved. But it is true here as well: a new approach always needs investment at first.

As long as you do not have your own local branch, it is important to develop good contacts and connections at a distance and to cultivate these, even independently of a concrete planning project. Creating trust and constant links with potential clients are fundamental but also necessary measures for gradually establishing yourself on the Chinese market. It is a good idea not to become too dependent on particular individuals here, but to cast the net as wide as possible.

As well as building up links with clients, you should also work with reliable service providers (plot service, model-makers, etc.) – not least because this keeps down the amount of luggage you need on your own business trips. Deadlines set for competitions are often tight, and it is usually necessary to send data and documents (e.g. for duplication) to Chinese service providers and to be able to rely on the quality of the documents produced in the mean time when you get there yourself.

Personal summary

Strongly growing global markets like China need a lot of classic planning services. We have to address this work alongside changing demands at home, to guarantee that our planning practices will continue to exist in the medium and long term. We have to draw on the factors that make us distinctive as European architects and engi-

Ill. 1.7: The fluent architecture of the East China Grid headquarters: a building en-
semble whose architecture reflects innovation and distinctive technological qualities is created by superimposing mature structures and future urban development.

neers, and that put us ahead of Chinese, but also other international
competition. Here I would identify, above all, innovation, creativity,
resource-friendly building, complex thinking and planning experience developed over many decades in the leading industrial countries and part of the sustainable capital we have accumulated. China
will definitely still have attractive planning work to offer Western
architects for ten more years.

I do not intend to lose sight of China personally. My connections with the country were and are too strong. I have experienced extraordinary situations in recent years that have taken me further in my personal development and given me a different perspective on global matters. It does not matter how you approach China, or what angle you view the development of the country and its cities from, this enormous country with its equally enormous cities contains enormous potential for danger, but also for opportunities.

About the author:
Werner Sübai works as a project partner for HPP Hentrich-Petschnigg & Partner KG in Düsseldorf. He studied architecture from 1983 to 1988 at the Bergische Gesamthochschule Universität Wuppertal. After graduating he worked from 1988 to 1989 in the Overdick und Pezinka architecture practice, and has worked for HPP since 1989, except for the year 1992.

C 2   Branches in China

Nikolaus Goetze

Almost all the world's most distinguished architects are now also represented in China and take part in competitions there, or are already working on projects. Despite the fact that the building projects tend to be very large, not all the internationally active practices in China have a local branch, with the status of a so-called representative office. In fact, the principal advantage of such a branch is that constant presence in China expands horizons and also means that competitions, reports and possible building projects can be spotted and assessed more quickly through proximity to current events. Chinese clients now increasingly see a branch of the architecture practice as a key precondition for possible work together.

For this reason, shortly before gmp started working in China we decided to set up a *representative office* of this kind in Beijing. We opened our first branch in October 2000, and there are now eleven Chinese and six German employees of our practice there. A branch in Shanghai followed in April 2004. This now has 20 employees, of which 14 are Chinese.

If a Chinese branch is to succeed it is essential that there is a balanced ratio of Chinese to German employees. A Chinese client expects to have qualified and experienced German architects working for him on the spot, just as it is indispensable for our German employees to be supported by their Chinese colleagues.

The employees in the gmp branches in China represent our practice in the first place, but they also secure participation in new competitions that are then processed in one of our German offices. They then present these designs to the client, along with the plans drawn up in Germany for current projects. Both our Shanghai office and the Beijing branch are looked after entirely by our Chinese partner Mr Wu, in consultation with the German board, which includes seven partners other than Meinhard von Gerkan and Volkwin Marg. Each of the Chinese offices also has a German office manager. Staff are assigned to particular projects to be realized in China.

Our German colleagues in China work exclusively as architects, while the Chinese staff are involved in the planning teams and also in office administration, such as bookkeeping or secretarial duties, for example, as it is essential to speak Chinese for these activities, and to have perfect knowledge of Chinese practices like taxation and labour legislation.

Some of the architects from Germany are very experienced, long-standing gmp employees and have already realized outstanding building projects in our German offices. They are supported by young, dynamic architects who see a stay in Shanghai or Beijing as a particular challenge to their careers. The German architects spend an average of two to three years in China before coming back to our offices in Germany.

As with the German employees, there is a balanced ratio of experienced architects to recent architecture graduates among the Chinese staff.

In order to promote good working relationships between the German and Chinese offices, we also offer Chinese colleagues of proven ability the chance to work for a longer period in one of the gmp offices in Germany. Our experience has shown that precisely this professional but also cultural exchange guarantees continuous quality in the handling of our many foreign projects.

Choice of Beijing and Shanghai as locations

gmp chose Beijing and Shanghai as its two locations, as these two large centres are developing into prosperous cosmopolitan cities at breakneck speed, and offer ideal conditions for branches of foreign architecture practices because of their international nature. Alongside the major events, the Olympic Games in Beijing in 2008 and Expo 2010 in Shanghai, competition between practices provides the necessary spur. A branch based in Shanghai will find it difficult to acquire projects in Beijing, just as a Beijing branch is unlikely to meet with any success in competitions announced in Shanghai. Also the two major cities and their populous environs offer a large potential for exciting building work in future years.

As well as this we must not forget that the airports in these two cities are ideal starting points for projects in southern China, in the case of Shanghai, and projects in the north of the country from Beijing.

It is not necessary to set up project-related, temporary branches in other Chinese cities, except for very large building projects. For example, this made sense for us when we were building the Shenzhen Conference & Exhibition Center: we won the first prize in the competition in 2001, and were then commissioned to do the planning work. We set up an office in Shenzhen in the building phase, used mainly by our German site superintendent while supervising the enormous project, for which about 255,000 square metres of built volume were completed in just under two years.

Chinese legislation lays down that branches of foreign architecture practices are admissible only in the form of *representative offices*. These are permitted only to coordinate, not to offer planning services themselves, which is why our designs, as has already been mentioned, continue to be drawn up in our German offices. The *representative offices* are also not entitled to place building proposals, and have to work with a prestigious local partner practice that holds a licence for submitting building proposals.

We either function as a master planner who co-opts the local practice into the planning team as a subcontractor, or for many building commissions the client may commission us to work on certain special phases. But from 2006, because of its WTO commitments, the Chinese government will have to issue planning licences to branches of international practices for the first time.

Legal basis

In China, employing international specialists for structural engineering or building services is usually confined to the preliminary design phase.

For very large projects, including, for example, building exhibition centres or opera houses, the specialist planners are also commissioned for parts of the final planning phase. But the local Chinese partner practices will handle all the further working phases. It is regrettable in this context that, given this division of responsibilities, it is not unusual for innovative approaches by the foreign engineers to be sacrificed to the routine solutions of the Chinese experts who are commissioned in their place.

The Chinese partner practice will also take over almost all the discussions with the approval boards, though the international practice will be invited to make a presentation to the board. In contrast with this, we are in frequent touch with the relevant town planning authorities and the fire brigade, as foreign experts are often asked for advice in this context.

Interfaces with specialist planners, local government departments and clients

But the most important aspect of the Chinese branches is the constant and intensive communication between the German offices and the local *representative offices*, which can be achieved only in this way. The geographical proximity of the two gmp branches in Shanghai and Beijing to our Chinese clients and the responsible authorities creates an important and irreplaceable basis of trust that prevents a great number of misunderstandings and offers the best possible conditions for providing the planning teams in Germany with concrete material for further work on the projects. But being so close also carries the risk that an undue number of meetings can dilute a planning process that seemed to be on target at first in the course of the negotiations.

Conclusion

Branches offer the best conditions for getting to know a country, along with its culture and the mentality of its population, and to create the close contacts without which excellent cooperation is generally impossible. But a branch does not just make communication easier, it also ensures that the desired quality is maintained. So the branch is all the more important the further away from the practice headquarters it is.

But it is absolutely essential for all the branches to be in close contact and communication with the architects' headquarters at all times. Exchanges of information and knowledge must be permanently guaranteed in both directions, in order to ensure synergy and quality within the office philosophy. Otherwise there is a danger that branches become increasingly independent and the name of the architecture practice suffers from inadequate quality brought about by a lack of control. On the other hand, work input from foreign architects who have already accumulated several years of experience in practices in their home country guarantees that the authenticity and originality of the head office is maintained in the Chinese branches as well, and the desired architectural quality safeguarded.

About the author:
Nikolaus Goetze studied architecture at the RWTH Aachen from 1980 to 1987. He was a member of Prof. Holzbauer's Master Class at the Hochschule für Angewandte Kunst in Vienna in 1985 and 1986. Since 1987 Nikolaus Goetze has worked for von Gerkan, Marg und Partner, since 1994 as associated partner and since 1998 as partner.
Projects he has realized include the Zürich Versicherung, Domstrasse in Hamburg; Ku'Damm-Eck, Berlin; Gerling Versicherung, Stuttgart; Guangzhou Development Central Building, Guangzhou / P. R. China; Luchao Harbour City, Shanghai / P. R. China; Shenzhen Convention and Exhibition Center, Shenzhen / P. R. China; Nanning International Convention and Exhibition Center, Nanning / P. R. China; Archives and Exhibition Halls Pudong, New District Shanghai / P. R. China; and the Palm Hotel, Dubai, United Arab Emirates.
Nikolaus Goetze regularly lectures on his professional activities in China and takes part in jury procedures and symposia about urban development in Hamburg.

C 3 Commercial viability of Chinese commissions

Quinn Lu / Michael Pruss

The Chinese planning and building market offers enormous opportunities to foreign firms because of its enormous growth potential. But a high degree of commitment and readiness to take risks are required to survive in this market. This chapter attempts to identify the factors that are important for the commercial viability of commissions in China.

First of all, the question arises of why foreign architects get contracts in China at all. One of the main reasons is the fact that foreign architects enjoy a good reputation in China, standing for high-quality and professional work. German architects, in particular, are a trademark for high-grade architecture and guarantee precise planning and design. Prestigious projects tend to be awarded to international planners and well-known international practices, who are thus paid considerably higher fees than their Chinese counterparts.

The mentality of European engineers conveys secure planning and a serious approach to the client. Although European architecture is rated more highly, Chinese tastes are predominantly inclined towards American building culture. European engineers are very much in demand for special prestigious projects and high-tech buildings, and by clients with international experience.

However, there is no lack of large and established planning practices in China.

There are over 10,000 state practices in China, some with 500 to 1,000 employees, who have all the necessary planning licences (see also Chapter B 2). These practices are former ministry design institutes (e.g. Ministry of Construction, Ministry of Aeronautics, etc.) or municipal and provincial design institutes (e.g. institutes of architectural design in Shanghai and Beijing).

State planning practices

As well as this, private engineering practices have been permitted since 1974. Licences (A, B, C) have to be applied for to set one up, and these are dependent on the size of the practice, its efficiency, professional experience and capital. Many practices are similarly structured to their European counterparts, and thus easier for international planners to deal with than the state institutions.

Private Chinese practices

Specialist engineers

Then again, there are very few independent engineering practices specializing in structural engineering and technical services planning. Specialist planners (services and statics) are usually part of the design office structure.

Scope of work required

Commercial viability issues

As the working plans and building supervision are almost completely in the hands of Chinese offices because of the licence system, foreign practices' commercial activities are largely restricted to competitions and design services. In order to test the commercial viability of a possible planning commission in China it is first of all essential to gain a clear picture in these phases of the remuneration to be expected and the time, effort and expense that will have to go into it.

Comparability with European projects

Given the particular features of the Chinese planning market it is fundamentally impossible to compare the treatment in depth of projects in China and projects in Europe or America. This is one of the reasons why many distinguished practices show a great deal of uncertainty when dealing with their first commissions in China, and do not bring projects off profitably.

Contractually agreed work

The nature of the work required is, of course, very important as a basis for possible remuneration. As a rule, the planning contract lays down precise descriptions of the job and scope of the planning operation (plan types, number of plans, planning depth, special services like perspectives and animations, for example), as well as terms of payment; it also establishes a time frame and a payment plan. Even though these matters are fixed contractually in China, they change constantly throughout the project, in contrast with many European countries. So when looking at commercial viability, greater flexibility and differing planning requirements should be taken into consideration.

Depth of treatment in the planning phases

The heading *design planning* in the contractually agreed work says very little about the actual work involved if this is compared with home projects. For example, design planning in China is much less focused on realization than in Germany or the United Kingdom, but the amount of effort needed for presentation is immensely high. It is also extremely rare for any work to be commissioned over and above the design: realization planning is handed over to local practices, so that for the foreign practice any realization planning that might be commissioned is likely to be confined to providing key details or advising the design institute, rather than covering and listing every detail of the subsequent process. Differences of this kind are, of course, relevant to estimating the amount of planning needed and should be considered before submitting a tender.

Travel and incidental expenses are a crucial factor for projects in China. As well as cyclical visits on the spot, dates are often arranged at short notice to deal with questions that have just been raised. These mean a great deal of travel if no local branch has been set up. If the foreign planning office intends to influence the design and implementation of the project in its later phases as well, regular contact with the locally based design institute is needed, and this is usually paid for only via a consultancy contract. Transport costs for models and planning material should also be taken into account, which is why many practices use services in China for model-making, brochures and the like.

Other cost factors

Fees

Independently of the practice's own commercial viability calculations, there are also Chinese fee regulations similar to the German HOAI (Regulations on architects' and engineers' fees) payment scale, but this applies only to Chinese practices and in many cases is taken only as a guideline and basis for negotiations.

Setting fees

It lays down fees for the various working phases in the fields of Architectural Design, Interior Design, Landscape Planning and Urban Development. The tables distinguish between building types (housing, public buildings, monument conservation, etc.) and building classes, which lead to three building categories relating to the extent of the planning work.

The greater the building volume, the lower the percentage calculation basis for the fee becomes.

As many foreign architects cannot readily ascertain the building costs because they are working only on design, or because the client does not always convey them correctly, a tender from an international practice is usually based on gross floor space or plot areas as shown in the masterplan, rather than on the actual building costs. International practices can demand higher prices on the basis of their higher demands and expectations. However, the incidental expenses must be calculated and included in the tender.

Basis for the fee

Fees are a matter of negotiation. Adequate room for manoeuvre should be built in at the start of the negotiations, so that compromises can be made if necessary. In the provinces, Chinese planning practices can command approximately 1–3 euro/square metre for housing construction and 4–8 euro/square metre for office/shop construction for complete planning services from preliminary design to working plans. In conurbations like Shanghai these figures rise to about 2–5 euro/square metre for housing and 6–12 euro/square

Fee negotiations

metre for high-quality office/shop construction. But the larger the building project, the more discount has to be given for quantity.

International planners can only claim 20–30 per cent of this sum for design services, as has already been pointed out, they are not permitted to provide planning services for authorization and realization purposes. However, they can demand up to twice or three times the fees paid to local practices, depending on the extent to which they are known, and their degree of distinction. A margin of 10–30 per cent should be costed in to provide room for manoeuvre. The conduct of negotiations differs considerably in the various provinces and regions.

Calculating fees

Calculating fees for the example of a high-quality office building in a major city is demonstrated below: an area of 30,000 square metres, for example, and a guideline price of 6–12 euro/square metre gives a fee range of 180,000 to 360,000 euros. If the proportion for site investigation through to design planning is fixed at about a quarter, then the fee paid to a local planning office would be approximately 45,000 to 90,000 euros. For a foreign practice, such fee levels can easily be doubled, making a tender sum of 90,000 to 180,000 euros possible.

Clients will not always work within this framework, but will try to negotiate on a lower base. Conversely, a prestigious practice can command considerably higher fees. The client's marketing strategy and the negotiating skills of all those involved are crucial factors. Consultancy fees for working plans and engineering services can be negotiated freely as a flat-rate fee. Here there are no clear guidelines; manner and sensitivity are the keys.

Payment conditions

Planning practices should always insist on an advance payment (10–30 per cent are usual), and ask for payments by instalment after services have been rendered. Here a detailed payment plan is negotiated in advance, structuring the payment phases sensibly. Plans should only be handed over after the advance or instalment payments have been made. Ignoring this rule presents a considerable risk for the practice employed. An element of risk remains that the last payment will not be made, so the final payment should be kept as low as possible. Court proceedings suing for money owed cost time and money, and may well come to nothing.

Currency

The fee should be paid in the appropriate foreign currency and transferred to an account in the planning practice's home country. As a rule the fee is agreed in dollars or euros, which minimizes risk in terms of the Chinese currency, renminbi. Transferring one's own capital out of China is problematic both legally and financially. Bureaucratic approval for transfer is very time-consuming. Hence there should be a contractual agreement about who is responsible for paying conversion and transfer fees, and how financial charges (e.g. VAT) should be handled.

Possibilities for profit

Drawing up urban development designs and concepts is a preferred activity for international planners. However, as a rule, this will merely cover the practice's own expenses and rarely makes a profit. But such planning work is not to be underestimated in terms of market presence and potential references. They are necessary if a practice is to acquire more profitable commissions for developing a concrete building design. *Schematic design* represents by far the largest part of the total fee (up to 30 per cent).

Initial investments

The foreign planning office should plan a long preparatory phase with appropriate investment when it comes to the first profitable commissions. The effort needed to find local partners, maintain contacts with clients and collect references pays off only for "healthy" practices that are stable in the market place.

Practices that are constantly present and position themselves well in the market also have a chance of acquiring direct commissions. Working on all the legally permissible phases from design development to consultancy on working plans offers a high potential for profit based on the size of the projects. It is to be expected that restrictions for international planners will slacken or even disappear in the next few years. But there is still little prospect that foreign planners will be able to establish a practice and take over final planning work in future. The present position is that foreign architects and engineers should be able to set up their own practices from early 2009, in other words five years after China joined the WTO.

Local presence

Cost risks

There are very few legal risks for international planning practices in the design phases. As a rule, there are no problems relating to Building or Liability Law. The main risk is losing fee payments, which can be minimized by paying attention to a few basic rules (see payment conditions). (See also Chapter B 2)

Chinese clients' payment morality differs greatly depending on their professionalism and experience in dealing with Western business partners. Care is advised in the case of effusive promises, as it is the world over. But large firms with international experience are concerned about their reputation and are no better or worse than

Payment morality

their Western counterparts when it comes to reliability in terms of payment.

New private companies spring up rapidly all the time. Construction companies merge and set up new firms. There is a danger of early bankruptcy for inexperienced, unstable companies, and thus the loss of outstanding planning fees.

Insolvency

Commissions from subsidiary companies of private developers who set up special project firms for building work represent a very great risk for architects and engineers. If negative signs start to appear, the company could be wound up under certain circumstances. Given a set-up of this kind, the basic rule in China is: never hand over engineering plans before the previous piece of planning work has been paid for!

Some companies are set up with the intention of accumulating money for investments that allegedly promise to be profitable. Architects are used here to draw up impressive plans and render perspective views for marketing purposes. Architects and planners should be on their guard against such firms, as it is not unusual for the developers and planners to be tricked out of their money.

Political changes

But in the case of public building clients, there is a risk that projects can be suspended because of changes in political direction. There are no obligations vis-à-vis the planners. This means that commissioned practices could lose the commission without compensation for their planning expenses.

Risks attached to competitions

Most commissions for important public buildings are awarded through competitions in China as well. A protection fee is charged for participating in state competitions, and a small flat-rate payment made when the design is submitted. The winner receives a cash prize, which is placed on account in relation to the subsequent fee.

If competitions are announced privately, care should be taken to establish that they are serious. For example, it can happen that no winner is named and the prize is retained, but the project developer retains the designs and could possibly realize one of them without the designer's agreement or participation. As is the case everywhere, competitions need a great deal of time and effort and are financially risky, but they are still necessary if worthwhile projects are to be acquired.

Conclusion

Breaking into the Chinese market with your own practice means investing a great deal of time and money. As the market is booming, many American and European architecture practices go to China in the expectation that they will quickly move into the black. China is certainly not an "Eldorado", but it is entirely realistic to expect a good position in relation to commissions, with interesting projects, if a client base is built up persistently and gradually. Just as on the home market, long-term, lucrative commissions are built up through a constantly growing network of contacts and connections.

The amount of effort needed to build a client base and the level of presentation are extraordinarily high by European standards. So any approach to China should be well prepared and accompanied by a good financial cushion to cope with any short-term failures.

Many European and American architects also underestimate the negotiating skills of Chinese building clients and developers, who are able to conduct tough, ingenious negotiations, but at the same time make it possible to establish long-term, faithful contacts. So it is necessary to come to terms with cultural differences in relation to planning costs and profitability, to understand them and to use these insights as a foundation for success.

About the authors:
Quinn Lu studied architecture at the University of Dortmund, Germany, and gained his Master's in urban development at Tshinghua University (PR China). From 1988–2002 he worked for PEP – Architekten, LTK und Obermeyer. Quinn Lu is managing director of the Werkhart International Group (Manager Office Shanghai).
Michael Pruss studied architecture at the Fachhochschule in Bochum. From 1999–2005 he worked as a planning architect for Erling + Partner, specializing in urban development and healthcare. He has been employed by the Werkhart International Group in China since 2005.

C 4   Working in Chinese planning practices: experiences

Gordon Brandenfels

Personal motivation

The Chinese building boom has not just made it possible for small and large planning practices to work on the Chinese market, it also offers individuals the chance to accumulate professional experience in China. Personal motivation for working there comes from a desire to get to know the culture, which is very different from Western culture, and its background in terms of planning history, and also because the building projects currently on the Chinese market are unique in their nature, size and diversity, and offer an attractive challenge to any planner.

There are a few things that should be attended to and organized before it is possible to work in China. This chapter deals with these, and with the normal working day.

Visa for China

Visa requirements for China differ according the country of origin, and the duration and concrete purpose of the visit. A business visa is needed for working in China. For this the usual documents are needed and also a letter of invitation from a state or state-authorized office. In the country itself, it is possible to apply for a working visa if you are employed by a company registered in China, and it will probably be issued for ten months in the first place. The company employing you should allow a period of about one to two months for the working visa to be processed. The business visa can be valid for a year, and the maximum duration for a particular stay is restricted to 90 days (sometimes there are changes here, so visas are issued for intervals of 30, 60 and 90 days' maximum stay). If all the documentation is available, a business visa can be issued via the express process (express visa) in a single day – but as a rule you should allow for a period of three weeks. Chinese embassies or consulates will provide detailed information about the documents and formalities required. A number of agencies also specialize in acquiring visas.

Health insurance

A private health insurance should be taken out for China, as generally speaking the European statutory health insurance schemes do not cover medical care in China, if you were not sent there by your employer. To be sure, you should make enquiries with your home health insurance provider.

When planning a longer working visit to China, it is possible to have a few important items imported by ship, in addition to the usual flight luggage. It is not at all unusual to rent fully furnished dwellings. In the large cities it is possible to live in housing estates occupied exclusively by foreigners. These are appropriated furnished in terms of lifestyle – but in general are very expensive. Another possibility is to look for accommodation on the open housing market, with the assistance of your employer. An acceptable home in Shekou, for example, costs 300 euros per month.

Accommodation

When working in China as a European or American, you have first of all to get used to different working conditions, starting with the size and design of your workplace. Often this will be in an open-plan office, divided by little screens into individual workstations approximately 1.5×1 metre in size. It is very difficult to work on large plans in such a little box. In my experience, the furniture, like chairs and tables, for example, is often very small as well, so that sitting down and drawing are very tiring each day.

Day-to-day office life

Another major difference is that the projects, usually housing estates, are often the size of a small or middle-sized town here. All projects are processed at enormous speed, with the intensity of the work fluctuating considerably. For example, a housing estate for about 3,000 people can be planned in a period of six to eight months. As the employees are expected to be constantly at the office's disposal, and work has priority in the way they organize their lives, there seems to be no need to take measures relating to good and sensible organization of work.

Putting a great deal of pressure on deadlines is very common. For example, changes of detail to a plan are discussed at a Friday evening meeting, and they have to be dealt with by Monday. Then there are often periods where nothing is done about the project at all. When this happens, it is normal for employees in large offices either to sleep during the working day, with little attempt at concealment, read the newspaper or simply chat to friends on the Internet.

The range of work available for Western foreign specialists is usually restricted to conception, preliminary designs, designs and drawing up key details. By allotting this range of work it is hoped that the foreigners' specific abilities will be put to good use, and that Western ideas will filter into the designs and thus make them more readily saleable.

Jobs for Western colleagues

Both the staff and the spatial structure of the relatively small planning Chinese office I started to work in are very different from the

Office structures

Western norm. With the exception of the proprietor, the ten Chinese employees were female, and had trained as architects, interior designers, agricultural economists or graphic designers. There were also three male Filipino colleagues who had studied landscape architecture. China did not offer landscape architecture degrees at that time.

The office consisted of a large room of about 35 square metres, divided into work cubicles. The foreign employees' desks were placed on the window side. The Chinese staff sat inside the room and worked by artificial light. Some discussions took place in the office proprietor's room. There was also one more tiny room without windows where the female accounts clerk sat.

The work in this office was organized by the office proprietor. He devised the design guidelines for projects as well as developing customer contacts. The Filipino colleagues and I were responsible for design work and elaborating details, while the Chinese women dealt with translating the hand drawings into CAD. Individual projects were usually directed by two experienced Chinese colleagues, as they were able to deal with outside communications.

The office worked mainly on outdoor facilities for large housing estate projects. The estates were designed by an architecture and urban development practice that cooperated with my office.

Day-to-day work

I was responsible for developing sketches of ideas for the outdoor facilities, which my Chinese colleagues then translated into CAD at enormous speed. The first project immediately demanded working out a concept for all the open spaces in an estate for over 5,000 people. I was not used to sketching out ideas without a computer – even sketches tend to be worked out almost exclusively on a computer in Western countries.

The shape of the working day was also exciting and new for me. The working day started at 8 a.m. and ended between 5.30 and 10 p.m. A five-day week was the norm. Overtime, at the weekend as well, was relatively normal. On weekdays there was a very long lunch break of one to one and a half hours, in which many colleagues went out to lunch. After lunch my Chinese colleagues brought out deckchairs or sleeping mats or simply pushed two office chairs together for a siesta. The office lights were often switched off centrally at this point. Once the lunch break was over, work slowly got going again. It was never possible to see exactly when the working day was going to end. Some days the staff went home at regular times, but there was often work to be done in the evening. Office work frequently ate into the weekend as well, as clients liked to fix Sunday meetings to catch up on how their projects were currently progressing.

By international standards, German graduates are pretty old. My Fil-ipino colleagues had graduated in landscape architecture at the age of about 21 (Bachelor) and by the age of 26, which is when I took up my first post in China after graduating, they had been working professionally for some time.

Age of new professionals

As I see it, the principal difference between Chinese and foreign workers is their approach to tasks or problems and the way they are handled. Chinese engineers are trained to produce a passable result as quickly as possible, while in the Western world personal creativity and individuality are promoted.

Differences between Chinese people and foreigners

Because of the lack of skilled workers in China, it is customary in architecture as well for employees to be wooed away after a very short time, or actually to start actively looking for a new job them-selves. Often employees have just familiarized themselves when they move to a competitor. Wanting to be better paid is a frequent reason for rapid turnover – the present employer is informed by his col-league that he is looking at a new job in which he will earn 15 to 25 euros more per month.

Staff turnover

Such problems did not arise in an Australian architecture practice in which I worked in China at a later stage. The staff were very well paid from the outset, and a bonus was added to the salary of a complete group of employees when a project was brought to a successful conclusion. Every employee was respected, and their work acknowledged – though on condition that they subscribed to the company credo. This meant doing everything necessary to provide the best possible service for the customer. To this end, all the staff were called together once a month to hear a talk by management about good architectural achievements in the company, and some that needed to be improved. Quality assurance in the company made absolutely sure that each employee felt responsible for his or her project. Another reason for there being very little staff turnover in this company was that it had a very good image.

But in purely Chinese offices I have seen the architects employed being compelled to work in the Shanghai winter at temperatures below freezing point in unheated offices with windows that were not airtight under incredible pressure of time, sometimes deep into the night. Some of them then tried to keep their fingers moving with hand-warming bottles that they kept next to their keyboards. If one compares these very different working conditions, it is possible to see the range of possible working experiences available to architects or engineers in China.

Salaries / payment

Western employees working in a local office in China are usually paid approximately 1,200 to 2,000 euros. This is well above the salaries paid to Chinese architects, which range from about 250 to 650 euros. A normal factory worker can keep himself and his family on his wages of about 50 euros per month – but the cost of living is considerably higher for foreigners, as their expectations will also be much higher measured against Chinese standards. A drink in a bar costs between five and ten euros, for example. Of course foreigners will not want to do without certain products like coffee, cheese and milk, which are very expensive in China. Cheese is imported from New Zealand, for example, and costs twice to three times as much as we would pay for it in Germany.

Prospects

Living and working as an engineer or architect in China enriches all aspects of life. You break down mental barriers relating to the feasibility of projects – while at the same time learning to live with new boundaries in terms of time and organization. Apart from the scale of the projects, which is incredible by European standards, it is the cultural experiences and the traditions that are still clearly discernible in the details of daily life that make a lasting impression and also put their stamp on personalities, as well as on an individual's own development.

About the author:
Gordon Brandenfels read cultural studies and environmental protection in Rostock and landscape architecture at the Gesamthochschule in Kassel. After graduating he worked in Shenzhen, which led to numerous contacts and competition entries. He has directed Brandenfels landscape + architecture in Münster, founded in 1973, since 2002; it has had a branch in Shanghai since 2002.

C 5 "Dos – don'ts"

Dr Bert Bielefeld / Lars-Phillip Rusch

As the personal reports show, there are many ways of behaving and various practices and customs, both in China and in negotiations with Chinese business partners, which can be crucial for the success of an involvement or the further progress of a project. Some aspects of negotiations are very different from practices familiar from the European and American building industries.

The reasons for this lie partly in the historical development of societies in the East and the West, and the understanding of individuality associated with these, but partly also in the general view of the importance of contracts and agreements. While tradition has from time immemorial shown each Chinese to be part of a society, Western culture places each person's individual freedom in the foreground. Experience shows that it is possible to comprehend the behaviour patterns that arise from this and to develop an appropriate understanding with increasing experience of dealing with each other, but it is well-nigh impossible to adopt them or to grasp them completely. But a general approach to dealing with each other should still be addressed. In China, in particular, politeness requires that the usual rules of manners there are followed and that insulting the host or business partner, perhaps even unintentionally, to the extent that he loses face, should be avoided.

In terms of social behaviour, business partners of a Western stamp are fixated on the result of the work. Activity is directed at solving any problem posed directly, and coming closer to and achieving the set aim within the previously planned structures and timescale. The Chinese, or Asian, approach tends to be determined more by the business partners being together. So it should always be a basic aim to create a friendly atmosphere of mutual trust. Aloof behaviour is misinterpreted by the Chinese as lack of interest and arrogance. Negotiations should be conducted patiently, in a friendly fashion but also toughly. Anyone who is too quick to move away from his positions or justifiable demands and gives in easily is seen as weak. Of course, the Chinese always work to the end of achieving aims, but the path does not have to run as straight as we are used to in the European or American business world. Many of our authors have stories of long discussions and presentations of their projects, carefully prepared in detail, that were ultimately granted more or

Negotiate correctly – achieve aims

less fleeting attention by their Chinese people responsible. Decisions were often taken not on the basis of the quality and content of the individual piece of work: on the contrary, the planner's prestige and previously realized projects were the most important matters. These factors, paired with enough social competence to take an interest in the potential client, to entertain him after the presentation during a long eating and drinking session, are the deciding factors for and against further work together.

American and European rules apply in China

Relying on assurances that this is how it's done, or this is not how it's done, is not only wrong in China, it is wrong everywhere. Of course rules that apply to working together in Western countries apply here as well. Discreet investigation of the Chinese partner before working with him creates a certain sense of security and can at the same time form the basis for a correct approach to a project.

In the case of contracts and other documents, the Chinese version is decisive in case of doubt, so this should be carefully checked to establish that it agrees with the English or German version. For this reason, the interpreters needed at negotiations have a special part to play. They must understand and convey the Chinese side's subtleties and overtones, and also adapt statements that have perhaps been translated too directly and thus seem impolite in the particular context. Often interpreters can be asked for advice in unfamiliar situations.

Preliminary work and remuneration

As the reports of personal experience show, it is never possible to predict precisely how a project will proceed, and since building ventures that are definitely going to be realized one day turn out to be completely impossible on the next, preliminary work should be kept to manageable proportions. It is highly advisable to agree realistic advances for planning services, and flat-rate payments according to the progress of the planning or building phases. Here the rule applies that the same precautionary measures that are used in other countries should be practised in China as well. When making commitments one should pay attention to limiting the use of time, staff and resources, and also to defining these limits precisely. The trick lies in using an existing basis of trust to find the right path between your own peace of mind and the client's requests and aims. Here it is often not the size of the project that is crucial, but its benefits to your own company. Small projects can build up a basis of trust and prove your own expertise.

Attempts by clients to influence the feasibility of a project by getting "big names" behind it, and thus putting the authorities under pressure, may be advantageous to them, but puts planners in a bad light in the eyes of the authorities.

"Undermining" the authorizing departments who are actually responsible in the context by splitting projects up or other masking measures does not achieve the desired aim as a rule. The appropriate authorities are aware of this approach. The legal position here is quite unambiguous.

The connections and contacts needed for successful activity on the Chinese market cannot be made through a single visit with the aim of possibly concluding the business. Regular visits, discussions and meals together create trust and strengthen personal ties. The Chinese always perceive these ties as being formed between people and not between firms or societies. This is considerably more important to the Chinese than a business relationship fixed on a piece of paper in a contract. A change of contact person for the Chinese should therefore be avoided if at all possible, or be made by very careful introduction of the new person. Maintaining connections, so-called *guanxi*, is the basis for business life in China. Such connections are built up and cherished throughout a person's life. Once accepted as a competent business partner and thus often as a friend, you can be sure of support as part of the group.
guanxi

Chinese people define themselves in terms of the success they achieve and the people they surround themselves with. Success achieved jointly strengthens the position of all those involved. It is not just the responsible client who is praised for a successful project, but the planners and the firms involved in the realization process as well. You are recommended to other people, and recommend people yourself, you forge more personal and professional links and can broaden your field of business.

Hierarchies are much more clearly defined than in the West and form the basis of the social order. Mutual respect in the family and in society between older and younger people and in the business world between management and workers is one of the basic principles. The obligations derived from this are always mutual: the person superior in status is responsible for the professional and private welfare of his employees and can expect loyalty from his colleagues for this. If either side breaks this rule the other side no longer feels obliged.
Hierarchies

Chinese business partners want to and must be "cherished". They expect to negotiate with partners of at least the same status. The highest-ranking person at a meeting is always the spokesman. He will make decisions and determine the course of the meeting. They deal with traditional matters like greetings or starting to eat. Of course, the guests are expected to behave accordingly: the highest-ranking guest must respond to the friendly words and praise the host, his friendliness and generosity. He will thus gain prestige ("face") in all eyes.

If someone calls you his "friend", this does not necessarily mean the same as it would in Europe. Business connections of equal rank often mean the same as a friendship for the Chinese. Friendly contacts should be cultivated: with occasional presents, invitations and favours. Requests can also be made in the name of friendship, and "these cannot be denied as a friend". "Friends" often mean *too* well with you, and are offended if you do not want to accept an invitation to a wild karaoke evening or a dubious nightclub. But if you do accept, it is expected that both parties will say nothing about anything that might happen.

Face

To the Asian mind, "face" means a person's reputation or standing. Success, generosity, composure enhance your own face. Confirming these things in others enhances their face and thus your own as well.

You should constantly be sure to maintain and enhance your opposite number's face at negotiations, presentations and celebrations. Social standing increases if you praise what they have done, their culture, their successes.

Small gestures are very important in this context in China: for example, the order in which people are greeted must correspond with their relative status. Business cards and presents should also not be handed over casually. It is a mark of respect to present both business cards and gifts with both hands, and to take them in the same way. Expressing an appropriate degree of admiration by examining the business card briefly enhances your opposite number's face. For your own information, and to help in learning the names of the people concerned, it is quite in order to make small notes on the card that make it easier to remember the person and also to place them correctly in retrospect.

Eating and drinking

Veritable "feasts" are often arranged to strengthen business contacts. Eating rates very highly in Chinese culture. So a potential client can be offended if an invitation is not issued, just as a successful evening accrues a large number of bonus points. A Chinese host will always try to fulfil all his guest's wishes. For example, there will always be more to eat and drink than is necessary. Trying to eat everything, which in Western countries is seen as a sign that the food has been enjoyed, is considered impolite in China and would cause a Chinese host to order more food so that he does not seem mean. Unusual and adventurous dishes are served, the best and most exotic that the particular region has to offer. Many bowls are placed in the middle of the table, and everyone helps himself with his own chopsticks. If you don't want to eat something it can be pushed discreetly to one side of your own little plate. The serving staff will change the plates at regular intervals.

Tips are not usually given, even at large business meals, where you might well feel you should reward the staff for their efforts and patience.

Expressing wishes that cannot be fulfilled puts the host in an embarrassing situation where he can lose "face". This should be avoided in all cases.

To the regret of many foreigners, excessive drinking is often associated with eating. Beer or wine is the principal drink in southern China, but in the north a strong rice spirit – *bai jiu* – is preferred. A glass should be drunk with at least the most important people round the table. Women are usually allowed to drink only beer, but the water that has been politely ordered tends to be seen as a slight affront. These insults can perhaps be transformed into sympathetic understanding through constantly reiterated excuses and justifications. However, it is a good idea to bring at least one person who can hold his drink to important business meals. Only health problems or religious reasons can be accepted as serious reasons for not drinking but should not be used as a glib excuse.

When the meal is over the guests are escorted to the door. Important personages should be accompanied at least to the lift, or even to the outside of the building. Everyone waits for the lift or the car together, and stays until the lift goes down or the vehicle departs. A brief handshake is a sufficient farewell.

Saying goodbye

All numbers except four are thought to bring good luck in China. The Chinese word for four sounds like the word for dying, and so the number should be avoided. The colours white and black, and dark colours, stand for mourning and death, while light, friendly colours symbolize success and happiness.

Colours and numbers

Conclusion

It should be pointed out that the behaviour, situations and rules described here are just simplified generalizations. There can be no recipe for dealing correctly and appropriately with every person and every situation. Here sensitivity, persistence and the desire and ability to become familiar with new situations are needed, and form the basis for correct behaviour. The Chinese are always interested in solving problems together, forgiving mistakes and thus achieving mutual success.

Our thanks to the authors for the many tips and suggestions for this chapter.

Progress reports

D 1   Planning commissions in China

Dr Bert Bielefeld / Lars-Philipp Rusch

It is a major step for a planning practice to develop a market that is over 10,000 kilometres away and whose culture, language and traditions differ greatly from its own. And yet the Chinese planning and building market exerts an almost magical fascination for foreign architects and engineers. Western architecture is very attractive to Chinese clients, which means that there are a large number of American and European planning practices on the spot, working to acquire Chinese commissions or carrying them out successfully.

There are many different ways of breaking into the Chinese market. Contacts with planning offices already working in China, networking trips or specialist excursions, personal relationships with clients and town or university twinnings have opened the door to China. Making a move towards China and following the path to success in China need an open mind, great personal commitment, and a sense of delight in one's own work.

The following accounts give an idea of some Western practices' experience with working in China. All the reports are written by employees, project managers or management figures who are responsible for directing projects in China. All the authors have accumulated personal experience of Chinese projects and give accounts of their day-to-day work.

The contributions also cover a wide range of different project types and sizes. Planning work may involve developing huge cities in the middle of nowhere, redeveloping and adapting existing urban structures to cope with ultra-rapid growth, planning and realizing skyscrapers, sports facilities or museums, building new detached homes with high-quality detail or painstakingly reconstructing and renovating historical building stock – whatever it is, the authors' experiences provide evidence of an immense bandwidth of planning possibilities in China. As well as this, technical expertise is in great demand. Building processes and building products that are part of a planner's everyday equipment in Europe and North America are just managing to take a firm hold as the market opens up.

There is nowhere else in the world where planning and building work is so diverse and so entertaining. Whether it is a little practice with a few employees or an "architecture factory" with numerous branches in Europe, America and China, the Chinese building market holds a lot of opportunities – but at least as many risks. We would like to present you with a whole range of views and approaches in this chapter, from global players to small and middle-sized architecture practices that have sought and found their way to China.

D 2 Von Gerkan, Marg and Partners – gmp

Nikolaus Goetze

Our activities in China did not start with a strategic decision, but came about as part of a series of happy chances: firstly, two completely different, unusual projects and then an architecture exhibition in Beijing.

Off to China

In 1998 we took part in a competition announced in Germany to build the German School in Beijing. We were familiar with the competition conditions and requirements, and also with the competition offered by our fellow German architects. Even the jury had only German members. But the country the school was to be built in was completely unfamiliar to us at that time.

The set building period was extremely brief, and all the competition entrants ridiculed it at first. But later we had to realize that this was just a little foretaste of the ultra-rapid tempo in China, unimaginable in the German situation.

After our design had won first prize and the Federal Building Ministry had commissioned gmp to realize the project, we started to get a sense of what a challenging adventure we were faced with: the German School in Beijing now had to be planned and also built, in the heart of China's up-and-coming, vibrant capital – on an island of German sovereign territory.

After a very detailed planning phase, Philipp Holzmann took on the job of main contractor, with the difficult task of realizing the project to meet the Ministry of Construction's ideas of quality in an extremely short period of time, working with gmp and the modest resources available in China.

But if the architects and project manager had not been dispatched to China the project would have been considerably damaged during the very difficult building phase: there was no end to the fights the team had to conduct with the Chinese subcontractors, who had hitherto been able to draw their experience only from mass housing construction, to ensure that every detail was finished to the appropriate standard. Often parts of the building that had already been completed had to be pulled down again until they finally reached the desired quality, which was then immediately reflected in the happy faces of the rattled planners and project managers. Bit by bit a school went up that was of extraordinarily high quality, by German and especially by Chinese standards.

It became clear to us only in retrospect that the client for this project and the building company from Germany, along with our familiar German building code, provided ideal conditions for realizing this building in China.

The first Chinese commission

The commission that now follows, the first purely Chinese one, realizing the Nanning International Convention and Exhibition Center (NICEC) was to demonstrate this to us in practice immediately.

Nanning, the highly hospitable capital of Guangxi province, announced an international competition for building a new exhibition centre in March 1999. After presenting the design personally, gmp was awarded the first prize in May. But shortly after this the governor responsible decided to change the site, so the original design had to be completely revised. Five new versions followed, then finally we were able to start negotiating the contract. It had still not been concluded after five days and three nights. But as a press conference had already been announced, the two sides decided on a "mock contract signing" in public. After the conference the "mock contract" that had just been signed was torn up and the negotiations continued.

Ill. 2.1: NICEC – Nanning International Convention and Exhibition Center, ill.: Jan Siefke

Ill. 2.2: NICEC – Nanning International Convention and Exhibition Center, ill.: Jan Siefke

When the contract to build the exhibition and congress centre was officially and finally signed, great banquets were held, accompanied by toasts to friendship, intended to put our future joint activities on a firm footing. Responsibility was accepted for defeats during these meals, and practical cooperation between architect and client could begin. The contract did not come out of the drawer at any stage during the five years it took to plan and build the NICEC. Instead, all problems were solved argumentatively but in a friendly fashion, usually over an evening meal.

In subsequent projects as well we found that Chinese clients always use these contract negotiations as a means of getting to know their contract partners better and finding out how they respond to stressful situations, how easily distracted they are, and how the partners ultimately act together vis-à-vis the large negotiating team.

We found another way into the Chinese market in a quite different but equally effective way: on the occasion of the XX UIA Congress, which took place in Beijing in 1999. Here gmp had its first opportunity to present its projects to the Chinese public in an individual exhibition. We organized a show of work called "Building for the Public" in the Yan-Huang Art Museum in Beijing, and about 600 Chinese guests came to the opening. Television made a feature about gmp, and we became known in China almost overnight.

Architecture exhibition in Beijing

There has been an omnipresent, euphoric sense of new beginnings as far as China is concerned for some time now in Germany: German-Chinese town twinnings that had been neglected have been revived and strengthened, diplomatic visits take place at the highest level

The Chinese planning market

Ill. 2.3: GDCB, Guangzhou, ill.: gmp

and business relationships that had almost been forgotten have been taken off the back burner and stirred.

Many are tempted to risk this adventure by hopes of a new mega-market, linked with unusual and interesting commissions. The difficult economic situation and the political standstill in Germany, along with disillusionment about a united Europe, may be other reasons. The question now also arises of whether China will rise to be a world power, or whether post-Communist economic strength will collapse after the initial euphoria. The first proposition is supported by the

Ill. 2.4: Shanghai-Pudong Museum, ill.: gmp

high growth rates that will continue because of the large internal market, so that China, which is still the world's largest developing country with an average per capita income of just over 1,000 US dollars, will soon become the 21st century's leading economic power.

But skeptics call China a bureaucratic "paper tiger" and prophesy that the system will collapse under enormous state debt. An additional factor is that China's joining the WTO in late 2001 further exacerbated the social fault lines that are already in place.

Faced with all this, the Chinese leadership never ceases to point out its successes since the country opened up economically and politically in 1978: foreign investors see the sixth largest economy and the third largest trading nation in the world as the most attractive commercial proposition in Asia. China's international recognition was also enhanced when it joined the WTO. However, the length of the accession negotiations does give a foretaste of the future partner: they lasted for 15 years.

The Beijing government notches up new economic growth records every year, rising to 9.5 per cent in 2004. Its currency reserves are the second highest in the world and stand at 600 billion US dollars at the time of writing. Of a population of about 1.3 billion, 200 million Chinese no longer live in poverty. A rapidly growing urban middle class is supporting consumption and buying homes, cars and other status symbols. By the end of the decade the Chinese economy will have overtaken Germany. In 2039 – the prediction has it – China will have overtaken the USA, despite the latter's own economic growth, which is also considerable. Further successes for China – not just from an economic point of view – are the coming Olympic Games in 2008 in Beijing and Expo 2010 in Shanghai.

This good news dominates the Chinese press, while negative headlines regarding political unrest, for example, are overlooked or not even published, since this is suppressed by the state and not allowed to penetrate to the outside world. The Chongqing reservoir project is a conspicuous example of omnipresent environmental destruction. Corruption and legal uncertainty to the point of despotism figure unambiguously among the location's disadvantages. The high growth rates sometimes have a deleterious effect on the building economy, as overheating in the economy leads to inflated building prices. To counter this, the government is currently halting major projects until the market has calmed down again.

One major danger to economic, social and political stability is the dramatically increasing prosperity differential between the rich coastal region and the poor provinces in central and western China. The rural population stands at 800 million, by far the largest proportion of the overall population. But as agriculture contributes less than 15 per cent to the gross national product, and farmers' incomes are stagnating, it is anticipated that there will be an increasing tendency to move out of rural regions, which will bring the already mounting population pressure in the cities to explosion point.

Since the 1990s, Chinese firms have dismissed over 30 million people, and joining the WTO further increased short-term pressure on the labour market.

But I feel that the current Chinese leadership under President Hu Jintao is pursuing the process of opening China up economically in a credible fashion, and trying to use obligations to the WTO as a political lever domestically, in order to put through unpopular reforms.

The government has shown prudence and competence throughout a number of crises, so that trust in positive development predominates and is further boosting the run on China.

Hope of a "super-market" that has still not been developed has lured not only the heavyweights in German industry, like Bayer, ThyssenKrupp, VW (50 per cent market share) and BASF, for example, to China. Middle-sized firms have also followed and are reinforcing German commitment to China, which has caused many people to proclaim the "Chinese century" in their euphoria.

Project acquisition by competition

The building commissions that gmp is currently carrying out in China are all based on competition wins. gmp has taken part in about 130

Ill. 2.5: Model of Lingang

Chinese competitions since 1999, and completed 10 projects so far. At the time of writing, 16 building projects are at the final planning stage, or under construction.

Each competition is preceded by an application process in which the participating architects have to provide evidence of their experience and projects that have already been realized in the particular field to which the project applies. This can be airports, for example, or hospitals, museums or skyscrapers. Then between four and ten practices are selected, as a rule, to take part in the competition. The fee paid can be up to 95,000 US dollars.

In this context the competition situation in Germany could be compared with the football league, while in China it is more like the Champions League, as all the eminent architecture practices from Germany, the USA, Canada, Australia, Japan, Great Britain, France, Italy, Switzerland and Holland are romping around there.

Ill. 2.6: Perspective view of Lake Lingang, ill.: gmp

This means that considerably more effort has to be made: as well as plans on large panels, models on the largest possible scale, perspective views and, increasingly, three-dimensional films as well are a must when presenting a design. It is now taken for granted that architects present their competition entries personally, which can mean suddenly receiving a communication that you are expected in China within 24 hours to take part in the presentation.

The jury usually has one international guest, but otherwise consists entirely of Chinese. It will usually decide on two designs, leaving the last word to the mayor of the community.

Architects' fees and economic viability

Foreign architects are expected to provide a preliminary design, a full design and then key details for the final plan and overall artistic management. A local Chinese partner practice is absolutely essential, and will be responsible both for final planning and site supervision. Other firms commissioned by the client will deal with invitations to tender and awarding work.

As a Chinese architect always acts as master planner and is thus responsible for service installation, statics, infrastructure, etc., as well as the actual architectural services, but receives only 2.5 per cent of the chargeable costs, architects' fees are very low in comparison with Germany. It is certainly true that a foreign office as master planner will receive a somewhat higher fee, ranging between 2.5 and 5 per cent of the chargeable costs. But because building prices are extremely low, at only a quarter to a third of German prices, the fee is well below the amounts usually paid in Germany. The fee situation is likely to become even worse for foreign planning practices in future, as a new ruling lays down that different fees for Chinese and foreign planners will no longer be permitted.

This makes it clear that our Chinese building projects, whether they have been opera houses, museums, skyscrapers, exhibition centres or airports, do all represent exciting challenges for gmp, but the profit is by no means proportionate with the effort and expense incurred, and so such projects are commercially viable to only a modest extent.

I feel that a foreign practice can only survive economically in China if it runs several projects and developments at once and knows how to exploit the resultant synergies, such as travel and full utilization of experienced teams, sensibly.

High- and low-tech building

Even though we have now been working in China for several years we are still impressed by the dynamism and speed with which even the biggest building projects are pushed ahead and completed there.

Ill. 2.7: SZCEC – Shenzhen Convention and Exhibition Center, ill.: Jan Siefke

An appropriate helping of courage and an ability to meet deadlines play an important part here, as well as high speed.

I am also constantly fascinated by the contrast between the antiquated building methods – managing completely without machinery, but needing a proportionately larger workforce – and the highly technical work for which the most recent technologies are used, as in façade design, for example.

We first experienced these seemingly retrograde building methods when working on the Nanning International Convention and Exhibition Center, which is a good example for many of our building projects in China. The pile foundations for the complex, which covers about 90,000 square metres, were sunk by countless married couples: the man drilled into the ground metre by metre with his hand tools, assisted by his wife, who pulled the soil up in a basket, and then provided him with something to eat and drink as well. The work went on for many days, and at the end of each day's work the man was brought up via a hanging ladder. The shell of the building was erected by inexperienced migrant workers from western China, who lived on the building site during the building period as if as a matter of course. Here talented improvisation compensated for the lack of craft skills. Much to our regret, this often shows in the structural quality of the building.

In contrast with this, extremely bold membrane structures were erected without difficulty with the assistance of foreign firms. Here the Chinese client spared neither expense nor effort in faithfully realizing, in every detail, the design the mayor had passed.

After the long planning phase, the intensive co-operation between client and architect usually produced a committed team that had successfully tackled all the highs and lows of a difficult building project, which ultimately also meant that gmp was commissioned to extend the NICEC – a rare gesture, as it is not unusual in China for additional building phases to be completed with the same planners, but without the foreign architects.

Partner practices and founding a local branch of one's own

When realizing a new project, gmp, as has already been mentioned, signs a contract to cooperate with a distinguished partner practice in the particular town. In this way, we have now worked with numerous local partner practices; their planning competence ranges from highly professional and committed to inexperienced or even one-sidedly profit-oriented. But we became involved in so many projects in China and were taking part in so many competitions that we soon needed to set up our own office on the spot. So we opened our first Chinese office in Beijing in October 2000. At the time of writing thirteen Chinese and seven German colleagues work there. As well as this, we opened an office with five architects in Hanoi in 2004, as a result of winning the competition for the new Vietnamese parliament building in 2003.

Legal security and questions of liability

We are constantly confronted in China with a "legal jungle" that is not easy to comprehend fully. This problem can only be solved if we, as German planners, enter into a planning partnership at the earliest possible moment. But, as we have already seen, this model raises the risk that the Chinese partner, after working with the Western architecture practice for a time, will persuade the client that it is possible to go on planning and building without the foreign partner. Ultimately, he will say, he has managed to learn enough from his experienced Western partner already.

Another problem comes in the form of liability for planning errors: German insurance companies will only cover errors made by the architecture practice they have insured. But Chinese clients usually commission the architects to be the master planners, which means that they are also liable for work done by their local partners, and this can become a risk that is difficult to assess.

Cultural exchange and differences in mentality

Words like "China" and "Chinese" put a glint in the eyes even of planners with no experience in this field. But once people have had some on-the-spot experience, they become a little more guarded and point out certain problems that are not to be underestimated: these are the differences in mentality, the foreign language, and then certain "misunderstandings" that crop up from time to time.

Ill. 2.8: Xinyuan Tower, Beijing, ill.: gmp

The Chinese mentality is very different from ours, and it takes several stays in Asia to begin to understand it. Europeans often act more emotionally, while the Chinese usually hide their emotions behind different behaviour. Here I am thinking of the Chinese smile, for example, which by no means always means agreement. Acknowledging this and being aware of it can avoid a lot of disappointment. Moreover, the countless compliments paid to us do not necessarily mean that the client is happy with our designs. The compliments are intended to convey his esteem and respect. So the phrase "no problem" often means that there are a large number of problems to be solved. Loss of face is something else that should never be underestimated. It drives the way in which all Chinese people act, and I have learned never to put them in a position where they may have to admit a mistake, or possibly not be able to reply.

As far as so-called "misunderstandings" are concerned, we have to learn that the reputation of European architects is used or abused to get round existing requirements laid down by the authorities. Thus, for example, one of our Chinese clients expected gmp to find appropriate arguments to double the area of a building volume that had been restricted to 100,000 square metres. Green areas needed in terms of urban development were to be built on, or fixed building heights exceeded by 40 to 50 metres. A foreign architect has to take particular care not to get in the firing line here.

It is also possible to realize how inexperienced some clients are because they set such tight deadlines. We have been asked to produce planning work that would take two to three months in Europe within two weeks.

But despite all the negative impressions described, the positive experiences should not be forgotten. Cities like Beijing, Shanghai and Guangzhou are becoming modern metropolises, but one still comes across islands of ancient, departed splendour that tell us a great deal about China's cultural past. And exciting cultural landscapes, as in Guilin, for example, help to create China's diversity.

Another very pleasant aspect is the exemplary Chinese hospitality, which is something we could learn from. We have often been met at the airport by our clients, and we have had company on many of our journeys. To say nothing about the lavish meals, where the really important decisions were actually made, after the formal discussions.

Conclusion

Since it has joined the WTO, China with its 1.3 billion inhabitants is an attractive business partner for the Western world, despite all the difficulties that can be encountered there. This is especially true for us architects: airports, railway stations, sports arenas, exhibition and congress centres are being built, not forgetting the many office and housing construction projects, which are of a size that is well-nigh inconceivable for us Europeans.

Cultural exchange in terms of ideas and working methods, paired with the economic dynamics of up-and-coming China, still represents

Ill. 2.9: New National Museum in Beijing, bird's-eye view, ill.: gmp

an exciting challenge, and I am sure that a market will develop for all services here in the future, and that the protectionism that still exists will give way to a liberal, open market.

Architects are increasingly acknowledged and respected as a profession. The European perception of architecture is reflected in China by increasing respect for sustainable buildings of higher quality.

About the author: see p. 102.

D 3 Philip Johnson Alan Ritchie Architects – PJAR

Stephan Jentsch

Getting into the Chinese market

Philip Johnson Architects has existed for over 50 years. The practice now employs over 100 people and has realized numerous buildings, interior designs and urban development projects in America, Europe and the Middle East. The practice is now called Philip Johnson Alan Ritchie Architects (PJAR), with its headquarters in New York.

The practice started projects here and there in China ten years ago, and more commissions followed quickly. It worked with a Chinese partner practice at first, but it soon became clear that efficient work to meet the practice's expectations would be possible only with employees on the spot. So a Shanghai branch was set up two years ago. At first the office did not employ many people, and worked on projects that had started their first phase in America. But a presence in China meant that new commissions were quick to follow, so now PJAR has 20 employees in China and is to increase this to 30 in the next few years. I have been working in Shanghai for two years now. I had personal reasons for moving to Shanghai: my interest in the practice's potential, and growth and change in China's big cities. The challenges offered by working here, which require unconventional answers, and the opportunity to enrich my Western view of architecture with Chinese perceptions about art and architecture, are just some of my arguments for living in China for a time.

The Chinese building and planning market

The growth of Chinese cities is impressive, and so is the speed with which their appearance is changing as a result of demolition, conversion and new building. Most commissions go far beyond those that most Western architects are familiar with in terms of their height, size, functional structure and speed of development.

In addition to this, the building industry is stimulated by special events: urban renewal schemes and numerous large buildings were initiated for the 2008 Olympics in Beijing, and EXPO 2010 in Shanghai is acting as a catalyst for the property market.

The building boom in the major cities has been going on for about 15 years, and will presumably boost a high demand for architectural services for a few more years. Demand for offices, homes and commercial buildings has now started to build up in the smaller cities (in China these are cities with 5 million inhabitants), as well as in the largest conurbations. There are enormous numbers of these smaller cities, often unknown in the West, and they represent additional potential away from the metropolises for the next ten years.

Most Chinese projects are on a large scale. Urban-scale planning is often linked with architectural development, and multi-storey buildings for various purposes are what is usually wanted, including of course skyscrapers. Building complexes or even individual buildings usually involve areas ranging from over 20,000 square metres to over 300,000 square metres. As well as this, landscape planning, design studies and interior design are commissioned from foreign firms.

The Chinese housing construction market is problematic for foreign architects. The very dense high-rise residential complexes (floor space index up to 5.0) are firmly commercially oriented in ground plan and façade. But these residential complexes are very lucrative for developers.

In China there are two main types of domestic architecture practice: the so-called Local Design Institutes (LDIs) cover the greatest part of the market. These are wholly or partially privatized businesses. They were originally allocated to a particular region, and this will still be their main business area today. But most LDIs offer engineering as well as architectural services. The universities have their own practising architecture departments as well, often made up of lecturers at the university, and they receive large numbers of commissions, regionally or nationally according to qualifications.

Planning practices in China

The second type are small and medium-sized practices, founded by the Chinese, in some cases with foreigners, and enjoying increasing success.

There are now large numbers of foreign firms operating in China. Australian architects were early on the scene, and they now have branches in several cities. Most major American practices have Chinese branches, and have already realized prestigious buildings. Very few European architects have offices in China. Most of them work with Chinese partners or send employees out at certain planning phases in a particular project.

The projects are comparable with the American market in their nature: building typologies (shopping malls, skyscrapers, etc.); closed high-rise residential complexes and a strongly commercially orientation involving dense structures in major cities are requirements we are familiar with from the USA.

Procurement and dealing with clients

It is essentially quite easy to start a project in China. The clients' enthusiasm and the large number of projects, with still relatively few competent and experienced architects, makes it simpler to procure projects at first than in America or Europe. But while it is possible in the West to estimate the extent to which procurement efforts will pay off and when a fee can be expected, in China the procurement phase can be more protracted. Unfortunately, constant uncertainty and changes in the basic conditions can be expected throughout the project.

We come across three different kinds of new client:

1. enquiries we receive through clients' recommendations
2. general interest based on our practice's reputation
3. clients who have found out about our practice for other reasons

We provide preliminary services in the form of brief suggestions about the project, moving on to the first studies. As well as this, we take part in competitions by invitation for which a fee is paid. These are relatively rarely large international competitions. Cities and municipalities have to put work up for public competition (nationally). Planning offices likewise request designs from a number of architects for projects affecting the cityscape. Both these variants are of interest to foreign architects only if the client invites the architect to participate directly. Numerous architecture fairs offer another opportunity for making contact with potential customers.

guanxi – connections   A great deal is said about so-called *guanxi*: these are in the wider sense personal connections for procuring commissions. Many Chinese architects have close links with certain sections of the government, municipal administrations, developers or groups of firms that have grown out of state companies. They regularly gain commissions from these firms, and have clear advantages there in competitions. If one comes across this kind of combination of circumstances when competing for a client or in a competition, it is rarely worth taking part. These *guanxi* are often overestimated, however. A foreign architecture practice can also build up a longer-term connection with a client within a manageable time frame through good work and personal commitment, though Chinese colleagues' abilities are often important as well.

As a rule, clients expect architects to start work on the project immediately, often before a contract or way of tackling things has been agreed. Chinese architects can produce complete preliminary designs very rapidly and efficiently, and foreign practices have to stand up to this competition. The client will not be persuaded to commission an architect until he has seen a design. But the first design is seldom final, and often it is a kind of study – though already quite detailed in terms of design – and the client and others involved in the project use it to make decisions about the size, purpose and, of course, the character of the project.

Communicating with the client remains an important factor throughout the project. An important feature here is taking an interest in and acting on the client's wishes, and understanding his ideas about style. This perception of the architect as the client's adviser is customary in the USA, while many Europeans in China come to grief by pursuing their own architectural ideas too single-mindedly.

Communicating with the client

Most decisions are made in the course of personal discussions, as many Chinese clients are not used to formal communication in writing. It is difficult to assess clients and their background. Involvements in terms of company strategy and political decisions often can't be understood until a project is under way.

We come across a lot of clients with little experience of construction projects because their company used to work in a different business field. Public funding authorities usually have long hierarchies, and decisions are postponed within these. On the other hand, municipal authorities can implement their wishes as clients relatively easily as there is no private land ownership. This is more predictable for architects than semi-nationalized or private firms, which can quickly clash with the building department.

If a project passes off successfully, further projects can almost always be expected, often from the client's business partners as well, or from associated firms. A client's trust can often bring an architect a lot of work; for these reasons many Chinese architects hold back from stubborn insistence on their fee. In China it is essential to consider whether insisting on a full fee might bar the way to future commissions.

Follow-up projects

We use similar contracts in China to the USA. This is possible because a great deal of architectural practice has been taken over from the USA. Descriptions of services, working phases and requirements are similar in this case, and many of our clients have already worked with American clients and know these models. Ways of payment and payment agreements are the same, but adaptations in terms of work done, fee and point of payment are often necessary for local, smaller clients.

Planning contracts

Payment is made according to phases of completed work in China, as in other countries. Here a higher rate, up to double, is customary for foreign firms in comparison with Chinese practices, on the grounds of greater costs and effort (working abroad, travel expenses, higher quality).

Consulting a contract lawyer who will check the contract for correctness and applicability is recommended in China. As contracts are drawn up in Chinese, it is essential to have them checked by someone with a perfect command of legal language.

In practice, far more problems arise in relation to contracts and to keeping them: elaborate contracts will tend to put some clients off, rather than clarify the scope of the work, as many clients see the contract as a reference rather than the basis on which the work is done. The relationship with a client could suffer if contract clauses are invoked in precise detail in the course of the project. Changes in the preliminary design in particular are difficult to frame in a contract. And on top of this, conditions such as size, functions and the basis for the contract change all the time.

Payment and commercial viability in China

The first phase of a project is difficult to calculate financially as the number of changes to the design are more likely to generate costs than the building's size or prestige. And the client is still uneasy about the success of the project, and so he will be more reluctant to pay fees for a design. Commercial viability in this phase is crucially determined by the foreign architect's experience. The point at which he refuses to do any more work without payment and how elaborate his presentation should be can only be decided case by case.

In later phases (schematic design/design development), various options are also developed, but the work is considerably more concrete. The work the practice will put in and the level of remuneration can be defined more clearly.

Commercial viability is a problem in the realization phase. Here the foreign architect works with a Local Design Institute (LDI) that is authorized to submit proposals. The amount of work needed to achieve the desired quality can quickly exceed the relevant proportion of the fee. Often the foreign practice acts solely in an advisory capacity during this phase of the work.

Wage levels are generally low in China, with the unfortunate result that the number of employees fluctuates, hence wages are supplemented by profit-sharing or bonus payments. Nevertheless, wage costs are considerably lower than in the USA and Europe.

Infrastructure like computers or similar equipment is as a rule more reasonably priced in China than in Europe or the USA; so are internal travel and computer-generated images or print media expenditure. But then rents in the major city centres are at least as high as they are in Europe. Employee travel should also not be underestimated, in our case to New York, and accommodation, expenses and travelling time have to be costed in, as well as the flights. This is a considerable factor in comparison with the other expenditure.

On balance it is difficult to make a general statement about commercial viability. It is probably wrong to call China a goldmine. There are a lot of projects, and returns are increasing, but this does not always show immediately on the profit side. Covering costs depends very much on the structure of the practice.

The much grumbled-about payment morality in China is certainly a problem as well, but it can be kept in check by experiencing and understanding a different business culture. As might be expected in a booming economy, profit can be made, but it must certainly be borne in mind that in China an architect is, to a certain extent, subject to the same risks as his client. Looking at the long term, the experience accumulated after a few years working in China is a bonus that makes the architect attractive to other clients, who may then be managed more reliably and professionally, thus making projects rather more secure.

Scope of work and putting plans into practice

The Chinese phase work in the same way as the Americans: starting with *schematic design* (preliminary planning), followed by *design development* (design planning) and finally *construction design* (working plans).

Like most foreign practices, our work in China currently focuses on the *schematic design* to *design development* phases, and on urban development projects. We also work on preliminary studies and on studies for the architectural, cultural and commercial background of the project. Since we opened a branch in Shanghai, we have been involved in the construction phase in China as well. In order to achieve the necessary detailing quality, it is necessary to be involved as actively as possible in the construction phase. Most foreign offices are not authorized to submit plans: a practice has to meet very high requirements to be granted this right. In China these include employing architects and engineers who are authorized to submit plans. Hence foreign practices are obliged to work with LDIs. We station our employees in the local office for the construction phase, so that they

Commissioned work phases

can prepare working plans with the colleagues who work there and monitor construction quality.

Implementing plans

The Chinese construction process requires a great deal of patience from foreign architects, as building work falls far below American or European quality standards. Many building workers are untrained hands, often migrant workers from distant provinces. Working plans in the detail we are accustomed to are rare, not least because such plans cannot be understood on the building site. Buildings are very simply conceived in terms of construction techniques, and neither the statics nor the façade structures are particularly elaborate. Details are usually adjusted to familiar construction methods. Developing and implementing a new detail means much discussion with the building firm, with possible withdrawal from the building process.

But our experience suggests that there are differences here as well. If the client is ambitious and the LDI good, buildings can be finished to a very high standard. High-quality materials like natural stone and glass are just as reasonably priced as labour-intensive on-site solutions, which are made possible by low wages.

Deadline pressures and timescales for work

Architects in China are faced with the challenge of having to complete designs with very tight deadlines. For example, within ten days we once designed a shopping mall with residential towers and a park, drew plans, created computer renderings, printed them, bound them in book form and presented them, along with a model. Discussions then revealed that the site boundaries ran differently, and that plans for a hotel were wanted, rather than residential towers. So we adapted the perspective design and the model, again in an impressively short time. This was then repeated twice in a similar way.

Rapid project realization is also a constant source of surprises. For example, I was involved in a project where the client kept urging us to hurry, and finally made detailed suggestions about the column grid. As it turned out, we had already started pouring the foundations, in order to save time.

Project sizes

The way the Chinese treat "bigness" is impressive. Gigantic urban development schemes and plans are completed very rapidly. Where we would need permissions from various authorities, here a mayor decides over dinner.

There is no private land ownership in China, land is leased to private individuals on a hereditary basis for 50 or 70 years according to the nature of the project. It is scarcely possible to predict what will happen after that. This system enables the government to pass infrastructure and planning schemes very rapidly. Projects can then be realized very fast, supported by cheap and to an extent uncritical credit granted by the banks. It is important to maintain a critical distance from the project and the client, but at the same time to offer the project serious support and interest even in absurd situations.

At a very early stage in one project we were surprised to find ourselves at a conference that was being broadcast live on various stations. The project was cancelled a week later for mysterious reasons. On the other hand one often works on projects that are agreed after nothing but a five-minute presentation and several hours of eating and, above all, drinking – which sometimes makes one wonder how seriously things are meant – but ultimately they go on to be realized rapidly and well.

Every potential client has to be taken seriously. This takes time, but experience is needed to be able to assess the situation correctly. Criticism and enquiries about the feasibility of the project are often seen as arrogance.

The relationship with the client, as described above, is very important. There is no doubt that it is not enough to sign a contract with a client and then not see him again until the presentation. Many clients like visiting architects often and at length. They will expect to have lunch together after a brief discussion of the progress of the project. After that it makes sense to visit some of the practice's completed projects. Dinner in a special restaurant will be rounded off by a visit to a karaoke bar. If there is time, this programme will be repeated the next day. This does not sound very professional to some people, but it must be remembered that many clients do not judge an architect by his work, but by the way he works with the client – and the way he eats and drinks as well.

This personal communication demands a lot of travelling time and dedication. In terms of European or American thinking about efficiency, a phone call or a letter would have been enough, but a Chinese client judges the degree of interest in a project by whether the architect and his colleagues are prepared to put in a personal appearance.

Branches
Most foreign architects set up their branches in Shanghai, Beijing or Shenzhen first of all, as a large number of projects are still planned in these cities or the surrounding area, and many clients have their company headquarters there.

Philip Johnson Alan Ritchie has had an office in Shanghai for two years now. At first we ran our Chinese projects from New York, but we soon felt it was necessary to make contacts and a qualified office available to our Chinese clients on the spot, which we could also use for procurement purposes. Chinese architects were involved in these projects from the outset. It was important to us to ensure that our work matched Chinese standards in terms of design, function and distinctive cultural qualities. For this reason about 70 per cent of our employees are Chinese, and they anchor our office's design and technology, as well as its language and culture in China. The

Ill. 3.1: Pennzoil Place, Houston, Texas, USA

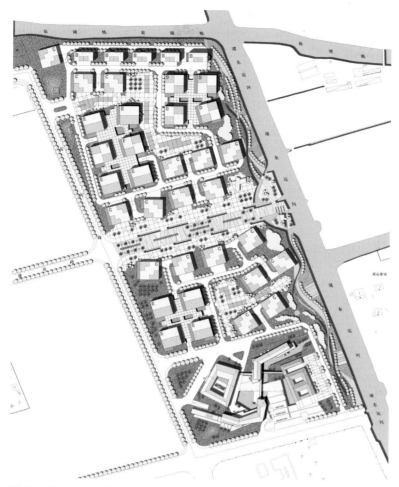

Ill. 3.2: Wangqiao project, masterplan

structure is flexible, and broken down into production teams, with foreigners and Chinese working together. We also station architects from New York in China temporarily for certain projects.

Legal questions and legal security in China

In my experience, a distinction has to be made when examining legal questions in China between the legal position and its application in practice. The legal system is fundamentally similar to the West for contract disputes. The contract fixes the court in which the dispute will be settled.

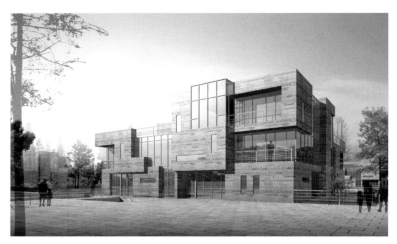

Ill. 3.3: Wangqiao project, business villa

Ill. 3.4: Wangqiao project, business villa type II

However, it is unusual to take a client to court over payment for services rendered, and such a case is unlikely to succeed. Such disputes are almost always settled out of court.

Insurance

Like most practices, we also have professional liability insurance in China. But as foreign architecture practices are rarely authorized to submit proposals, the risk of doing any harm is very low.

Ill. 3.5: Wangqiao project, office complex

As well as this, our Chinese employees have to be insured: health insurance, pension schemes, etc. have to be partly funded by the employer.

Personal résumé

I came to China over two years ago. Previously, during my stay in London and later in Holland, I was in touch with projects in Eastern Europe and China, and I felt that a lot would come out of keeping an eye on developments there and involving myself through my own work. Further motivation for working in China also came from the sluggishness of the European market and the impression that it would be easier to put my ideas into practice there than would be possible in Europe now.

The first step towards understanding China is to be aware that you understand nothing. Despite awareness of China's geographical and cultural coherence, developments so far have been marked by fragmentation and discontinuity. This is one reason why compromise replaces clear decisions today. The linguistic form tends to be the fundamental observation rather than the personal opinion, and a metaphor is often declared to be consensus. In China, rational lucidity is seen only as one possibility among many. China is currently schizophrenic by nature. While Western thought is reflected everywhere, China is also trying to rediscover her shattered roots. While modern skyscrapers are destroying old structures, shopping malls are disguised as ancient temples. The fractured image of the present, lasting only for moments before it shifts into a different form, is both construction and deconstruction at the same time; demolition is more permanent than the building itself.

Falsification becomes the subversive value of an unfettered economy set against the ancient illustrations of politics. Architecture is a mirror of this development: buildings and cities represent brief projections of needs and desires in the hurtling midst of change.

Presentation of sample projects

The following projects give an impression of our work in China in recent years. We can look back on a long tradition of building in the

Ill. 3.6: Ghiri project, bird's-eye view

Ill. 3.7: Ghiri project, tower 1

USA, but in China we are in a comparatively early phase. But projects develop rapidly, so two of the projects described are already under construction.

ACCU in Wangqiao is an urban development scheme followed by an architectural design for a plot near Shanghai. The programme provided for an office complex, catering and about 30 free-standing buildings that could be used as small office buildings or divided into four units as apartments. The only building on the plot was a 96-year-old house.

This house was to be crucial to the development concept. We decided with the client to keep the building and restore it. This gesture

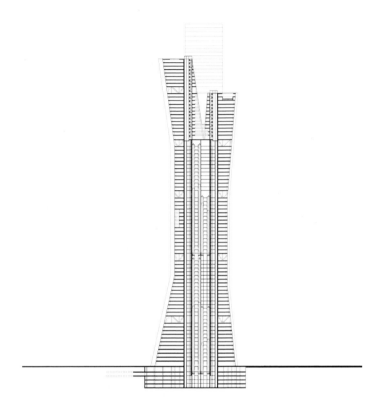

Ill. 3.8: Ghiri project, diagram section tower 1

of respect for old structures was intended to enrich the new architecture, as an alternative to the usual demolition.

The office complex took over the courtyard principle from the old
building: the offices, which are closed, semi-open and completely
open, form a courtyard. The 30 individual buildings were called
"business villas", to indicate their possible function as offices or
apartments. This openness of function caused problems with the
façade structure. As almost all the internal walls were variable, the
façade became the focal point, not the space. So the concept made
the façade itself into space. Protrusions and recesses, different materials and indented loggias and balconies made the façade a spatial
phenomenon.

Ill. 3.9: Shi Han Road project, bird's-eye view

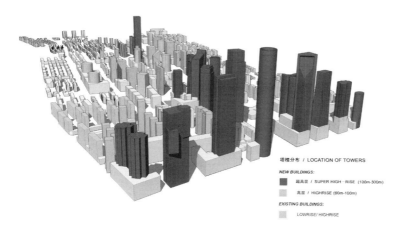

Ill. 3.10: Shi Han Road, height development

Three different types of material, stone, wood and glass, formed urban groups, and thus developed typical areas. Semi-sunken car parks under the groups created neighbourly squares.

Invitations to enter a competition for designing twin towers in Guangzhou were issued to international practices in 2004. Two towers were to be designed on a central axis in a newly planned CBD. The building that was developed consists of three towers that have

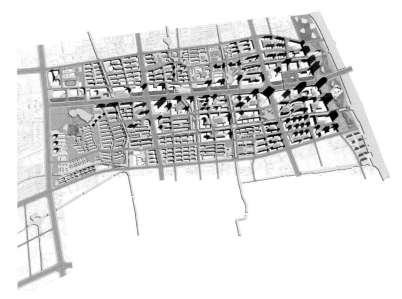

Ill. 3.11: Shi Han Road project, masterplan

grown together in the central area. This structure meets the difficult demands for use, area and lighting. Skyscrapers are always symbols on the city skyline, and in China in particular the need for iconographic form shows in decorations on the façade and the roof. The challenge was to design a characteristic building, convincing in its simplicity and functionality.

Shi Shan Lu is an urban development project in Suzhou, near Shanghai. The client wanted to analyse and restructure a 2.3 square kilometre area along a major road. The road forms a connection with the city centre, and is at the same time centre of its own area. The urban development is meant to represent a sign of some necessary re-thinking. Respecting existing structures conserves resources, retains the identity of a district, and creates the dimension of continuing time that is essential for urban systems.

About the author:
Stephan Jentsch, Dipl.Ing. architect (NL), works as Senior Architect/Project Manager for Philip Johnson Alan Ritchie Architects in Shanghai. He studied architecture at the RWTH in Aachen and the ETH in Zurich. While studying he gained practical experience in Prof. Gottfried Böhm's architecture practice in Cologne. After graduating he worked for the KPF practice in London, at eea (Erick van Egeraat) Architects, Rotterdam, and as a partner for MADA s. p. a. m. (Architects), Shanghai.

D 4   Romses Architects

Scott Romses

Travel and the exhilaration of seeing a place with fresh eyes is extremely stimulating to our work and growth as architects. Being transplanted out of one's culture, comfort zone and place into a new land and culture is like seeing the world through a child's eyes. This state of inquisitiveness and curiosity is where you want to be as an architect. Our work in China allows us to observe, test ideas, and operate at a scale and speed undreamed of in Vancouver.

I suppose these factors are what drew us to working abroad in China in the first place, and today they continue to preserve our interest and long-term commitment to working there. Yet, while there has been considerable media attention and hype on the emerging market in China for architects, those thinking about entering the market should not do so as a "get rich quick" business plan, or with lofty ideals based on conquering the next frontier of 1.3 billion people. To succeed, you have to be committed and in it for the long haul, as well as being sensitive to their culture and business practices. Yes, there are tremendous opportunities there, but for every successful venture there are also the unfortunate ones that wasted enormous amounts of time, money and effort to no avail.

How we got started
Before explaining how our firm started to work in China, one must first understand the conditions in Vancouver that made this a relatively natural progression in the growth of our firm. First of all, Vancouver is a port city strategically located on the edge of the Pacific Rim, and it benefits greatly from this geographic advantage. As a result, China and other Asian countries greatly influence all aspects of our society and culture. So the notion of working within the Chinese culture and business system was already familiar territory, since, in demographic terms, Vancouver and our client base largely consist of Chinese residents. I think Chinese clients, seeking foreign expertise, have a high comfort level in working with Vancouver firms, and consequently a strong network of architects and landscape architects has emerged who are very active in working throughout China. Secondly, the fact that our currency is slightly weaker than the US dollar – alongside our perceived political reputation – has

been said to add to our competitive advantage over our American neighbours.

Our first project in China came as a result of these circumstances and out of a casual referral from the close network of architectural firm already working there. Our firm was casually approached to collaborate on a prestigious project for an entertainment centre/hotel in

Ill. 4.1: Entertainment Center and Hotel, Qingdao

Qingdao. At the time, Vancouver was quite slow for architects, so the prospect of working abroad on a large-scale prominent project was very exciting and exotic. That was ten years ago, and we have never stopped working there since.

First impressions of the Chinese market

At the time of our first project in China, I had no idea that I would be here today on a return flight home from Harbin, China, writing this report after what is my 25th trip to the country. That first project was, at the time, just an exotic interlude between the many local projects we were working on in Vancouver. Yet that first trip to Qingdao and Beijing not only opened my eyes to a culture on the cusp of immense international influence, but also to a potential market for architects unknown in the West. I returned home excited about the success of the project, but even more so about the potential offered by the Chinese market which would allow my firm to expand the scale and focus of its architectural inquiry.

Our firm has since made a firm long-term commitment to pursuing foreign work in China for various reasons beyond economic gain, and it has managed to have a Chinese project ongoing in our studio continuously since that very first collaboration ten years ago. As a result, I now feel much more experienced and informed about the magnitude and potential of the Chinese market for architects. It is true that the opportunities there are probably greater than anywhere else in the world right now, but one must be careful not to be seduced by all the hype and the scale of building happening there right now. For me, it is more about seeking quality rather than quantity. There are endless developments one could pursue, yet the ones that contain

Seeking quality rather than quantity

Ill. 4.2: Beijing Elite Clubhouse

all the necessary ingredients to be inspiring, culturally relevant and memorable pieces of urban design or architecture are rare indeed. In line with my personal beliefs and goals, I consciously seek out those rare projects that offer this potential, as I am all too aware of and disturbed by the number of developments that merely fill space in the city, making little or no long-term contribution to the fabric of the place, to the life of its inhabitants, or to the environment. If I wanted, I could easily forget about pursuing local projects in Vancouver, and instead follow a career working exclusively in China. Yet for me, the balance of our foreign and local work is what defines our firm's study and practice of architecture, in the same way that the type and quality of clients and the intellectual challenge of the projects dominate our pursuit and selection of projects in China.

Contracts and competitions
Issues surrounding contracts are probably the most important factor when contemplating working in China. Most architects will have probably heard the "horror stories" of other architectural firms who have either not been paid, or have even gone bankrupt over disputes and problems surrounding working there. While we have generally escaped any such major contractual problems, we are certainly learning from our mistakes regarding the pitfalls of an ill-conceived contract. It is at best naive to enter into an agreement to work in China, assuming that your client will conform to the business and professional practices you are accustomed to in the West. One has to try and understand the cultural and business practices in China in order to have any hope of enjoying a healthy long-term working relationship there.

Since a typical Chinese project tends to not proceed linearly, with many changes and unforeseen issues emerging along the way, one has to be very careful to try and predict and protect oneself contractually from these departures from the original scope of work. Furthermore, many foreign firms spend a great deal of money and time travelling to China to try and secure a contract, only to find it not materialize after all these efforts. The art of negotiating an agreement takes great patience and willingness to participate in their cultural nuances of negotiation, as well as understanding the differences of their business culture.

Evaluating competitions   Competitions are very common yet they have a particularly troubled reputation for architects. In Canada, we have extremely clear and strict guidelines for what constitutes a competition – all in an effort to establish a level playing field among the competitors. In

China, the rules and parameters of competitions are very inconsistent and seem to be much more unpredictable. It is common knowledge that connections are one of the foundations of business culture there, and many competitions have been rumoured to have been won based upon this subjective practice. It is for this reason that I am very cautious about entering a competition there. However, the premier projects in big cities like Beijing and Shanghai tend to be awarded through official and legitimate competitions. Yet there is also a whole tier of competitions below these prestigious projects that are conducted less professionally, and it is these that I am much more wary of. When being approached to participate in a particular competition, ask a lot of questions about its nature, and one usually gets a sense very quickly of its legitimacy and whether it is just an excuse for the developer to seek cheaper fees by "dangling a carrot" for the work.

Special characteristics of the client

Any successful project, regardless of where it is located, requires a client/architect relationship based upon trust, honesty and integrity. When working in China, the fact that you are typically working with your client for the first time, let alone having to deal with the differences in culture and language, often makes the relationship seem unfamiliar and mysterious. It is for these reasons that it is essential to enter the Chinese market first in an effort to build meaningful long-term relationships. Chinese business culture is based predominantly on face-to-face contact and relationships. They are potentially as insecure and cautious as you are in working together for the first time, so the quicker you can establish a level of trust, and even friendship, the sooner you will succeed in working there.

The majority of my relationships with clients in China are perhaps atypical. My firm is often hired by a managing architectural firm in Beijing, whom I have known and worked with on many of our projects there. In over ten years of working with them, we have cultivated a high level of trust and a meaningful friendship, which alleviates a lot of the worries of working there. This unique client model is essentially a two-tier contract/client one in which my firm subcontracts directly to this managing firm, who, in turn, contracts directly with the actual client for the project. There are pros and cons to working in this type of arrangement, but these would be far too lengthy to mention in this brief report.

I think in terms of the unique characteristics of clients in China, you have to be careful not to stereotype who the "typical Chinese client" is. Each is as unique and diverse as any of your local clients might be. However, some common characteristics do tend to emerge. First, don't be surprised to see a relatively young client walk through the door when you first meet. Many of the people in high-level positions are part of a recent generation of highly educated foreign-trained individuals who have returned to China to assume such high positions. Second, my initial preconception was that the high-level positions were very much an "old boys' club" dominated by males. While this is still partially true, it is encouraging to see women now attaining very high-level positions in business and governance. Perhaps the greatest typical client characteristic for me has been the high degree of support and encouragement we receive to pursue contemporary and creative solutions within their projects. By comparison, our Vancouver clients tend to be much more conservative than our Chinese ones. I think China is trying very hard to emerge and be perceived in the world as a forward-thinking modern society, and this trickles down through all levels of their society and to the creative expectations of their projects.

Types of contracts: planning vs. building design

As previously described, contracts can be a difficult and time-consuming aspect of any project. Yet because your professional standards of delivering a project in your country may differ greatly to those in China, the contract becomes a key "bridging" document, clarifying for both parties what the expectations are. Therefore, I cannot emphasize enough the care and rigour needed in

Ill. 4.3: Silvercity Commercial Village, Dongying

Ill. 4.4: Silvercity Commercial

drafting these documents, in order to avoid disputes and problems through the course of your project. Part of the challenge in drafting contracts derives from the all too common fact that clients often provide very limited information describing the site, programme, scope of work, and regulatory requirements for a particular project. In Vancouver, it is the professional obligation of a client to provide such standard information to the architect prior to commencing, whereas often in China we are provided with a rough sketch of the site boundaries and told to "do whatever we think is best" for such things as the building programme. This obviously creates a lot of insecurity, and it takes time on your part to generate the programme and the parameters for the project. I tend to not recommend doing this, as it potentially exposes you to liability later on, should some of your assumptions prove incorrect.

Site planning contracts can be difficult, as I've found there to be a wide range of expectations for these types of projects. Be careful of the Chinese expected norm of charging fees as a cost per square metre. Architecture and planning is not a *product* or *thing*, like flooring that can be charged on a per square metre basis, but is rather a creative *service* or *process* that should be charged out based upon a thorough understanding of the scope of work. If possible, it is useful to try and find out about these typical cost per square metre charge-out rates, so you can use them as a reference for your own fee calculations. Another big potential source of contractual disputes derives from expectations of the level of detail to be achieved during the early stages of a project. For example, a "Concept Site Planning Stage" may mean rough hand-drawn diagrammatic solutions, whereas to your Chinese client, this Concept Stage may be a much

Site planning contract

more detailed package of CAD drawings. Save yourself a lot of grief and time trying to second-guess your clients on what they mean or expect at such stages of the work by requesting reference drawings of other similar projects to illustrate clearly the resolution expected.

Building design contract   Building design contracts in China are similarly often derived on a "per square foot of buildable area" basis, and the same warning comments made above apply. I avoid using such factors to generate a fee proposal – basically, I charge very close to what I would charge if the project were being done in Vancouver, and I then add on a certain percentage to account for all the extra communication and coordination time required for the fact that it is being done in China. Furthermore, it is inevitable that you will be expected to travel to China on numerous occasions during the course of a project. Sometimes it is hard to predict how many and how long these trips will be, so be sure to separate out the associated fees for these trips from your base fees. If your client has a standard contract he insists you follow and conform to, it would obviously be prudent to ask your lawyer to scrutinize such documents carefully prior to agreeing to anything.

Reimbursement for the Work

Getting paid for your work is perhaps the biggest anxiety of working in China. We have probably all heard the stories of those who have "been burned" working there. The fact that your client is halfway around the world doesn't make you sleep any better at night when you haven't been paid. On this issue we have been very careful, and fortunately have not had any major problems. There are a few things we insist on with regards to payment that help to protect us. Firstly, always ask for a retainer prior to starting any work. We have had no problem asking for and receiving at least a 20–25 per cent retainer upfront. Secondly, break your scope of work into small identifiable stages, and request that payment be received in full prior to delivering the associated work within these stages. In simple terms, the client will not receive the drawings until you have been paid. If your client insists on holding back some fees at the end of the project, be sure to minimize the amount of this final payment as much as possible (5–10 per cent of total fees), because it is this payment that you are most likely not to receive if a contractual dispute arises.

It can be a bit complicated for your client to wire you payments in your foreign currency. They typically need government approval to wire funds outside China, and certain corporate and banking protocols must be in place before such funds can be issued. Be sure to make certain such provisions have already been put in place by your client prior to starting work; otherwise you could be faced with lengthy delays as you wait for the bureaucracy to process your client's financial protocols.

The American dollar is often the benchmark currency used by Chinese clients with regards to fees. So be very careful on long-term projects should the currency value fluctuate significantly during the course of the project.

Expenditure and economic gain from projects in China

When we first embarked on these foreign projects we were relatively naive about what they entailed and how much we should be charging for the work. We did not do very well financially on those initial projects, but, having learned from our mistakes, we are now doing considerably better. We are not getting rich on these projects, and I suspect people entering the Chinese market go into it with these intentions. For me, the financial gain is only a secondary factor in doing work there.

There are certain "costs", both personal and professional, that one must weigh against any potential economic gain derived from these projects. These projects place heavy demands on my involvement as principal of my firm, as most of my Chinese clients insist on my direct involvement and my presence on trips abroad. So, because they are not easy projects to delegate to others in my firm, this puts pressure on my local work and client relationships. Furthermore, on a personal level, the numerous trips to China put a potential strain on my family life, as they occupy considerable time away from home. These are part of the costs of doing business there, and also some of the reasons why I limit the amount of work we do there at any given time. Also keep in mind that these projects move at a very fast pace, and this in turn exerts pressure on your staff output, requiring long hours in order to meet very tight deadlines.

"Costs", personal and professional

Range of projects

Every aspect of Chinese society is experiencing rapid growth, and consequently, a wide range of projects are open to foreign involvement and expertise. Whether they involve designing the planning strategies and infrastructure for a new town, or a highly specialized museum project, there are opportunities for whatever aspect of the profession you are interested in. Our firm specializes in both urban design/site planning, as well as the design of distinct speciality buildings.

Ill. 4.5: Tiger Beach Development, Dalian

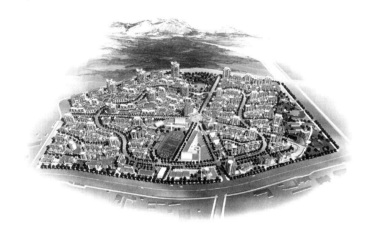

Ill. 4.6: ShandongTao Masterplan, Qingdao

Residential masterplans

Perhaps the majority of projects being conducted today entail residential development. The tide of migration to the cities is fuelling tremendous growth of high-density housing developments in every major city across China. Our firm has been responsible for several large-scale residential planning projects, and we are currently working on a 130-hectare development in Harbin. It is in these planning and urban design sectors that I feel Western expertise is most effective. Our experience of sustainable and green principles, coupled with our experience and interest in promoting rich, diverse and multifaceted urban environments greatly improves the status quo in China of uninspired, monotonous residential communities.

Ill. 4.7: International Competition Qingdao International Airport

The emergence of dynamic urban centres such as Shanghai and Bei-jing has established a strong awareness of the importance of plan-ning and urban design in the modernization of China's cities. This has in turn influenced other urban centres throughout China, with numerous urban design competitions and projects being announced. The public realm of the city is one area that requires great improve-ment, and architects and landscape architects are leading the way in this regard. Our firm has been fortunate to collaborate on some key urban design projects, such as the international competition for the new Qingdao Airport and surrounding lands, and a proposal to re-configure and reinvigorate the prominent public space, Xidan Plaza, in Beijing.

Urban design

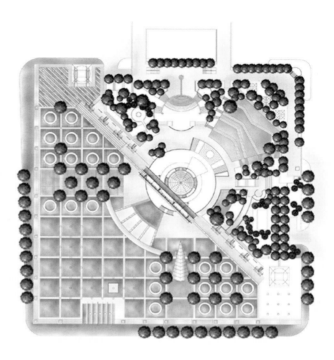

Ill. 4.8: Xidan Plaza Reconfiguration Concept, Beijing

Speciality buildings

While we enjoy working at the scale of the city, we also focus our efforts on creating bold and innovative solutions for important public buildings. The Chinese are known for embracing modernism, and one only has to drive around a city like Shanghai to realize this. However, in my opinion, they tend to look too closely at Western architecture, and instead are creating pastiche cities and buildings, comprised of "cut and paste" ideas from other Western cultures or architectural magazines. With every new building design project we become more familiar with the culture, place, and people, and hopefully we help them realize buildings that are more relevant to their needs and culture.

Residential building design

Great improvements have been made in housing in the last ten years in China, and as the emerging middle class becomes more and more affluent, so too does their desire for larger and more comfortable dwellings. Still, because of the need for extremely high-density housing, the challenge is to make these new developments as livable, healthy and socially stimulating as possible. There are some very specific and unique housing requirements particular to China that any foreign architect must research carefully if they want success in this market. To simply transport Western housing models to their society would not be well received. Over the last ten years we have designed numerous high- and low-density developments which have been well received because they balance the positive aspects of Western housing models with the cultural norms of Chinese society.

Special characteristics of project execution

It has already been mentioned that speed is a major factor in being able to work in China. Their culture prides itself on getting things done fast, and this also applies to the architectural process there. Buildings were typically executed in very large state-run architectural institutes, where a building's design and construction drawings were prepared very quickly. You only have to drive through any city there to see the negative results of this expedited process. So we spend a lot of time trying to educate our clients on the need for more time in order to produce quality buildings. Yet, today we still find the time issue the biggest constraint and challenge in the process.

Speed

Secondly, communication takes on a much greater role in the process compared to a typical project in Canada. Ideally, you have to have a good project manager in China, who can communicate with you on the daily questions, facilitate the flow of information and drawings between you and the client, and help you find your way through the various codes, planning and other governing information related to your project. Technology has helped us greatly in this regard, with e-mail, web conferencing, FTP sites, etc., but in the end nothing beats a face-to-face or, at least, telephone conversation. Geographically, the time zones of Vancouver and China work out very well for us, in that the end of our working day coincides with the time when they are waking up to start work. In a sense, the project "never sleeps" – someone is always working on it, either in Vancouver or China.

Communication

Another unique and potentially problematic aspect to the work is the fact that the construction drawings of any particular project must be prepared by a local registered firm. Therefore, you typically only get to work on the design and have to appoint others who carry on with the work after the design phases. It is therefore valuable to research who are the good firms locally, and sometimes you can persuade a client to retain the best ones in order to maintain the quality and integrity of your design ideas.

Lack of control over final product

Collaborations and affiliation with local firms

Collaborations are an integral aspect of our methodology and philosophy. Over the years, we have fostered and associated with a multidisciplinary network of talented firms and individuals who share our enthusiasm and energy in pursuing design excellence. Furthermore, these alliances enable us to expand our core team to meet the demands and needs of our most challenging projects. Our work in China is typically conducted in this collaborative manner to meet the often challenging constraints typically associated with these high-velocity large-scale projects.

Furthermore, it is very important to try and set up a collaborative relationship with a local firm in China. We have such a relationship with a firm in Beijing who are very helpful in getting new projects, managing the project, and collaborating when needed. Ideally, you want to try and find someone you know of and can trust, or who at least comes well recommended by other foreign firms working there. Try to find a firm that will complement your philosophy, type of experience, and especially, have the time and available staff to give you the support you will certainly need.

Legal issues

Fortunately we have not had any legal problems in any of our projects, and while it is probably true that business is generally less litigious in China, you must still do your homework to make sure you are not exposing yourself in any way. Since so many foreign companies are now working in China, there is quite a lot of information available on the issue of legal matters. Furthermore, there are numerous firms who specialize in international law.

It would also be advisable to let your professional institute know about your plans to work in China, as they will probably be able to assist you with understanding any legal and professional issues you may be exposing yourself to. The bottom line is that you will undoubtedly be working on very large projects involving many people and large sums of investment capital, so you must not become complacent about these matters just because the project is on the other side of the world. As a lawyer recently pointed out to me, just because the project happens to be located in China does not mean that a client there can't sue you here in Canada – these things do happen.

Liability problems and insurance

Perhaps the biggest issue surrounding liability is due to the fact that foreign firms typically only do the design drawings, while the local Chinese firm undertakes the construction drawings and construction supervision. Therefore, one has to be careful not to assume liability vicariously through the actions of these local firms. I suppose if it ever went before the courts, most or all liability would be transferred to the local architects. Yet, it would be prudent to spell out clearly in your contracts the limitation on your liability due to this issue. Like most architects, I am concerned about maintaining the integrity of our designs, as they are completed in the construction drawing and construction phases by the work of these local firms, so I often try, at least, to review and consult with these firms while they are finishing off the project. This, too, potentially opens up the possibility of liability exposure, and should be clarified in a contractual clause in your contract.

Furthermore, you must be sure to notify your professional insurance provider of any work you plan to do abroad, as this may affect your policy and, in some cases, you may not even be covered for such foreign work. In our case, our insurance coverage rates actually went down slightly to account for the fact that our liability exposure was less than if the work were done in Vancouver. This is all related to the fact that our involvement is typically very light in the construction stage.

Personal view on working in China

The fact that I continue to work in China, ten years after that first project in Qingdao, clearly demonstrates my continued interest and commitment to working there. As stated earlier, the financial gains and tremendous market there are only part of my reasons for staying involved. On a personal level, I have come to enjoy and learn greatly from the people and my experiences there. I never cease to be amazed at the magnitude of the changes in progress, and I am totally convinced that China will very soon dominate every aspect of all our lives, be it business, culture, the arts, politics, etc. However, as they embrace this change and become a more mobile urban society, this will exert great pressure on their social fabric and environment, so it is greatly rewarding to make a positive contribution that will help minimize these pressures. I really think if you are serious about getting into the Chinese market as a foreign firm, you have to act now. In the short period I have been working there, I have noticed a great increase in their expertise and design abilities: there will come a time, in the not too distant future, when they will no longer need our help.

About the author:
Scott Romses is principal of Romses Architects in Vancouver, Canada. He is respon-sible for the Vancouver office comprised of an inter-disciplinary team of eight staff capable of projects of varying scales and complexity. Scott received a Bachelor of Arts from the University of British Columbia, and a Master of Architecture degree from the University of California, Los Angeles, where he was awarded First Prize for his design thesis upon graduation. After graduating from UCLA, he spent two years working under Thom Mayne and Michael Rotundi with the acclaimed firm Morpho-sis. Since returning to Vancouver, besides fronting his Vancouver office, Scott has taught several design studios at the School of Architecture, at the University of British Columbia. Scott has received numerous awards for his work in both Los An-geles and Vancouver. He is also currently very active working on projects throughout China and collaborating with other architects, landscape architects, and urban de-signers for various projects there. While much of his work is at an urban scale, he also purposely seeks out, and focuses on, smaller scale speciality projects to support his ongoing interest in craft, materiality and construction. His work has been exhibited in various galleries, including the large group show, Artropolis, in Vancouver.

D 5   Bruno Braun Architekten

Bruno Braun

Architects have to work in many different fields, and these differ equally from country to country. The more alien the culture is and the more different the rites, forms and formulae are, the more marked the contradictions and the misunderstandings become. As people often start work with no idea and a good helping of undue self-confidence and conviction that their own experience can be applied everywhere, they do not usually recognize these differences immediately, and contexts are understood only step by small step. They gradually gain the insight that it is no good drawing comparisons with what they are familiar with and starting again from scratch every time. A schematic approach can help when finding one's way around in a familiar environment with a similarly conceived commission and comparable partners, but international architectural work has to be thought through in different cultural contexts. Projects are carried out differently in legal terms, the planning and building phases are different, and so, no less importantly, are the motives and mentalities of the clients and the general gestures of the building process. So it is exceptionally difficult to cooperate with clients, those involved with building and with architects on the spot, but it is essential, as it forges important links that make communication possible between all those involved, and these are essential for an idea and planning to be realized.

I would like to take the examples of a detached house in Beijing, a hotel and office building in Liu Lin, far away from any contact with the West, and restoring and converting a medieval courtyard complex in the middle of the historical city of Pin Yao, to show how projects with Chinese partners can lead to despair and an immeasurable amount of effort, but also to incredible new experiences and perspectives.

Projects in China

My practice has built in a variety of countries for years. Usually the client was from Germany, or we were preparing plans for German companies who were setting themselves up abroad. We are differently committed in China, because all the clients are Chinese, and the work has been done with Chinese partners.

Ill. 5.1: Pin Yao

Detached house in Beijing

Our first commission in China was a "piggyback" acquisition: an acquaintance was doing business with a Chinese trading company. He was asked to suggest a German architect to build a detached family home in Berlin. After a visit from the client in Germany, where some properties were viewed for reference purposes, we quickly agreed that it would be possible to work together well. Several visits to Beijing followed, with discussions about the spatial programme, functionality, building plots and preliminary sketches.

A very private atmosphere developed, including parents, siblings and friends as well. Nothing resembling a contract was ever concluded, nor did we even talk of one.

Carrying out the commission

Our long discussions fixing deadlines, plans, concepts for materials and colours were considered binding. The final plans were drawn up in Germany and produced on a scale of 1:20 or 1:10 with all the information in English. Direction of work on the spot was handed over to a Chinese architect as master planner. His office checked our plans to ensure that they met technical requirements, local laws and standards, and was responsible for the craftsmen and labourers working on site, and for keeping to the agreed deadlines. The German architect became a kind of "general site supervisor". The client was responsible for selecting materials for the individual trades. So I travelled with the entire family clan for several days, visiting the

Ill. 5.2: A DIY store in Beijing

well-stocked "building centres" in Beijing and surroundings, found
the desired building materials and ordered the appropriate quantities according to the agreed dimensions.

Surprises occurred all the time. Either the materials did not ar-
rive on site or they were transported inappropriately and were un-
usable, or the timber ordered for interior finishing was delivered as
untreated trunks, which were then processed by migrant building
workers in a simply equipped carpenter's workshop on site.

All the interior finishing, the furnishings and equipment in the
house, which offered about 500 square metres of living space, had
to be planned and fitted. Many transportable parts were chosen in
Germany, shipped to China in containers and assembled on the spot.

Originally the Chinese client, who was educated in New Zealand,
wanted a Mediterranean-style villa – an imported product looking
entirely to the West. After a great deal of persistence and persua-
sion to include traditional design rules and elements from the newly
emerging architecture, we successfully talked this internationally
successful businesswoman into acknowledging and accepting typical Chinese building culture in the interior and for the furnishings
and fittings. So Chinese antiques are now placed alongside modern
furniture.

Design requests

The house was handed over after a building period of almost two
years, including a few stoppages. The completed house in Beijing
attracted attention and led to further commissions in China.

Company headquarters in Liu Lin

A new headquarters for a private Chinese mining company is currently being built in the small town of Liu Lin in Shan Xi province, roughly halfway between Beijing and Shanghai in a westerly direction.

The company headquarters, originally developed by a Chinese planning practice, consists of an office and administrative area with a congress and training centre attached. The group of buildings is completed with two 21-storey residential towers, intended for a selection of the company's over 5,000 employees.

In this way a new site shaping the area's urban development is emerging in the remote provincial town of Liu Lin, in the centre of a mining area with open-cast work and coke manufacture.

Together with a forestry initiative and the construction of a large reservoir, this large-scale operation is intended to recultivate the landscape, which has been very badly damaged by the mining operations, and thus provide evidence of the company's responsible approach to the region. I was commissioned by the client to redesign the company complex in 2003, via private contacts and on the basis of small reference projects in China.

Working with the company's management team, the spatial programme was rejigged, and the existing building structure analysed

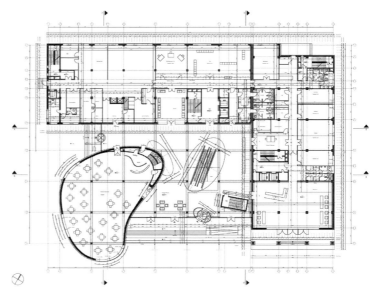

Ill. 5.3: First floor of the company headquarters in Liu Lin

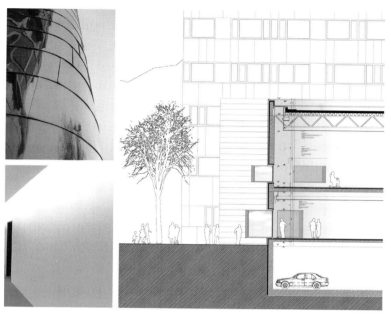

Ill. 5.4: Detail of the conference room in the company headquarters in Liu Lin

and examined for possible changes. The organization of the office areas and hotel functions were thoroughly examined. The entrance area and the congress section for 1,000 participants were completely redeveloped. The architecture of the building's outward image and the interior design were redefined and proposals devised for designing the façade.

Intensive consultations in China and joint excursions to sample projects in Germany were needed to familiarize the Chinese delegation with European standards and approaches, and to satisfy their desire for knowledge and to have their requests met. It was easy to agree when choosing materials to consider Chinese regional materials and their traditional uses, but the client wanted a European look for the interior.

Communication between planner and client

We provided the complete preliminary and final plans for the highrise buildings, the whole interior and the movable furnishings. Because English is not commonly used in the provinces, all the plans and information needed for realization were prepared in Chinese characters. All the discussions and written correspondence had to be translated. The important, direct mode of communication with the client and his colleagues suffered as a result of this. The constant presence of an interpreter means that nuances of gesture and intonation are lost. This caused considerable problems in the early

stages of the work. Cultural differences, the frequent lack of knowledge of building techniques, and the very different temperaments of
the people involved could often not be overcome through the filter
of translation, nor be discussed in detail. Essentials were often lost.

It was only with time and constant observation and comparison
of gestures, listening to the tones of the language, and with the
aid of spontaneous line drawings and perspective diagrams that we
were able to reach an understanding even without interpreters and

Ill. 5.5: The building site in Liu Lin

Ill. 5.6: Migrant workers live on the building site

establish the trust between client and architect that is essential for effective work together.

It proved extraordinarily difficult to work with Chinese architects on the spot for this project. The client had entrusted individual planning practices with different tasks, but all the plans and information came to them from Germany. Then a different practice was responsible for the façade from the office dealing with the shell of the building. The technical specifications were compiled by a Chinese engineering practice from a design drawn up to German standards and adapted to the conditions, standards and laws of the local situation for the building process. Yet another "part general contractor" with his own planning team was responsible for implementing my working plans and design concept. Difficult and also time-consuming coordination was needed, demanding a great deal of patience from the entire planning team. Often there was a sense of "competitive thinking" between the individual partners, involving sensitivities and sometimes ignorance as well. So some instructions were not carried out properly, and a great deal of effort was needed to put this right: staircase details were transposed, floor heights arbitrarily raised without considering adjacent parts of the building, etc. Here it was astonishing that the client never reprimanded the person who made the error in front of "the whole team", despite the fact that it was quite clear who was responsible. The reason for the mistake was

Working with Chinese planning practices

Ill. 5.7: Risky routes

always investigated at a late hour with a small group of people, and a great deal of fuss was made over assurances that it would never happen again. But no decision was ever taken about who should meet the cost of repairs.

Interruptions and transport problems

The building process is constantly interrupted by power cuts and for other commercial, political and inexplicable reasons, and site visits that have been fixed are cancelled at short notice. Here it should be explained that the journey to Liu Lin is an adventure in itself. The roads in the province are permanently choked with lorry transports for the coal and coke, and the many bridges are completely overloaded. Serious traffic accidents, enormous damage to the roads and collapsing bridges are no rarity, and have often meant breaking off a journey.

Despite all this, the shells of the buildings were almost complete by July 2004. The natural stone slabs for the newly developed façade were manufactured in a quarry in Mongolia. The outdoor facilities with reservoir and bridge were then almost compete, and work started on the interiors in autumn 2005. Completion is expected in November 2006.

Renewing a historic courtyard complex

Pin Yao World Heritage site

Another project in hand at the time of writing again required a quite new level of effort. The brief was to restore a 17th-century Chinese courtyard complex in the town of Pin Yao and convert it into a hotel. Pin Yao is a completely preserved 17th-century town with an intact town wall six kilometres long. And it is not just the buildings that have been preserved and have survived all the cultural revolutions undamaged: it is believed that the way people live and work in the town has hardly changed either. Pin Yao is a world heritage site and is now being carefully opened up to tourism.

Dealing with historical building stock

I was able to take on this project because of my experience in dealing with historical building stock in Germany. Hitherto, next to no attention had been paid to old building culture in China amidst the enormous boom in new building, but recently more and more state institutions, private building owners and the public have started to take notice of historical complexes and individual buildings. But there is often a lack of expertise in dealing with the existing building stock. Here years of experience in Germany can help, though not every restoration can be approached on a basis of direct comparison: special or traditional techniques practised locally have to be studied and researched. One advantage in Ping Yao is that traditional craft skills are still available and can be deployed to help with restoration. Exciting and entirely extremely effective ways of working together have developed in the course of this project.

Ill. 5.8: The courtyard building in Pin Yao

The plan here is first to examine the building substance and record this in plans showing its state at present, then to plan a small guest house or hotel for 25 people with a conference area, small restaurant and the necessary commercial facilities.

We are responsible for all of this; the client has designated a team of responsible technicians on the spot (from mining and craft firms), and they will put the plans into practice in consultation with us.

Planning brief

Ill. 5.9: The "workshop" on the building site

Ill. 5.10: Roofers in Pin Yao

Ill. 5.11: Ground plan of the guest-house in Pin Yao

Extended visits by colleagues from Germany are planned in this context. This is possible in the little town of Ping Yao, and given an expert client no local architects are needed for this conversion.

Work is due to start in spring 2006.

Conclusion

After six years' working in China it can be said that planning and building in China is an extraordinary experience. Encountering a completely different culture, an environment so different that it is almost impossible to examine, and direct contact and dialogue with the people of this country make creative and technical work uncommonly exciting and varied.

A high degree of acknowledgement and acceptance of concepts and design proposals gave me a great deal of creative freedom with the client. But the real limits tend to be reached in terms of incompetent techniques and craftsmanship on the site, inexperience, and also sloppy execution. It would drive a meticulous client mad to try to keep to the same levels in terms of precise finish, standards and technical building regulations as applied in Europe. But fortunately improvements are already detectable. This is one of the reasons why foreign architects are appointed more frequently.

Commitment to China needs patience, empathy and a readiness to deploy one's skills and competence as advice, rather than pedantically. Patience and a touch of calmness are definitely needed.

About the author:
Bruno Braun set up his architect's practice in Düsseldorf in partnership with A. Triet in 1979. BRUNOBRAUN ARCHITEKTEN, Düsseldorf, was founded when the partnership was dissolved in October 2003. The practice's activities include planning for building activities of all kinds, specializing in buildings for public and private administration, industry and commerce, restoration, redevelopment and conversion for historical and listed buildings, including church buildings and buildings for health and care in particular (spa and rehab clinics, old people's homes and special facilities for the handicapped and dementia patients). Bruno Braun is a member of the Bund Deutscher Architekten BDA and chairman of the BDA in Düsseldorf since February 2002.

D 6   HaiPo Architects – HPA

Kerstin Hartmann

HPA Architects is one of the oldest leading private architecture practices in Shanghai, and as such we have been able to observe the changing market for almost 15 years. Increasing market penetration by foreign architects is making competition on the architecture scene more demanding, diverse and exciting, but also harder. This gives us the opportunity and the challenge to place and assert ourselves within an ever-widening field of possibilities.

About the HPA practice

The HPA practice (HaiPo Architects) was founded in Shanghai in 1993, under the name HPGI (HaiPo Group International). The two partners Paul Chen and Haiqing Wu studied architecture at Tongji University in Shanghai and then did a Master's course in the USA. After ten years of study and working in practices in California and New Jersey respectively, they decided to return to China, which was already booming in the early 1990s, and to found a practice together in Shanghai.

At this time the market was overwhelmingly dominated by the great state architectural institutions, as setting up a private practice was not allowed in China until the 1980s. Very little trust was accorded to young architects who, as yet, had no projects to show in China. New commissions came only with references. On the other hand, there was a lot to do: after the country was opened up in 1976 and the difficult learning curve of the subsequent years had passed, the economy had finally liberated itself from the inflation spiral in 1990 and was ready to grow and build cities. So HPGI were able to find a developer who was ready to take the risk of working with inexperienced architects. The project, the Shanghai No. 2 Novel Department Store on the busy HuaiHai Road in the former French Concession, did not seem lucrative enough to the large architectural institutions, as it had "only" seven storeys and filled a relatively small gap in the buildings; they preferred to concentrate on large, prestigious projects. All the better for Chen and Wu, who had finally got their hands on a real building commission with this department store, and so would enhance their reputation with other clients. Chen and Wu could now land other contracts, with the No. 2 Department Store in their pockets. So in subsequent years their work included three high-rise office blocks in the new Hongqiao commercial zone and some shopping and leisure complexes in and around Shanghai.

In order to submit plans to the city for building permission, the so-called Grade 1 Licence is needed. It is still issued very rarely, and so it was necessary to enter into partnership with a state institution, in order to be able to use their licence. The partnership and friendship with ECADI, the largest Shanghai planning institution, lasted for a long time. Many of HPGI's early projects were also handled by ECADI specialist engineers.

HPGI also felt the effects of the 1997 crisis in Asia in the form of a considerably reduced number of contracts. The practice had to be slimmed down. The market recovered in subsequent years, and building started up again. The practice had 24 employees in 1997, by 1999 it was 45, and 60 by 2002. We now have about 100 employees. Of these, approximately half are architects, the other half interior designers, engineers and administrators. In 1999 HPA acquired 49 per cent of the insolvent ZhongFu architectural institute, which meant that a Grade 1 Licence passed into the practice's possession. Since then we have been able to offer a complete planning service, including all engineering and interior design services.

The office structure has grown over the years and follows only very rough rules. Unusually for China, HPA does not have any strong and obvious hierarchies. All employees are on an equal footing, at least on paper, and there are no titles like Junior and Senior Architect. Even so, the employees are divided into experienced and registered architects and younger college graduates. Something else that is unusual for China is the average length of time people stay with the company, which is over two years. Some of the longest-serving colleagues have already been here for over ten years. This is explained by the family atmosphere in the office, presided over by the two partners Paul Chen and Haiqing Wu. Communication flows very directly through these two men.

I was the first foreigner to be accepted by the practice, in autumn 2003. I didn't hesitate for long when I was offered the opportunity of living and working in Shanghai for a time. Contact with my Chinese colleagues at HPA means there is something new to be discovered and learned every day. This leads to very fruitful collaboration for both sides, so in the meantime even more foreigners – Europeans and Americans – have joined us, and will continue to do so.

After over a decade of planning activity, HPA has earned itself a stable position on the Shanghai architectural scene. We too have to

Internal office structure

Competition with foreign practices

Ill. 6.1: The department store is on a prominent corner between the HuaiHai shopping street and Maoming Road.

adapt to the fact that more and more foreign architects are settling here. Despite Chen's and Wu's US qualifications the practice is perceived as a local one and has to stand out for qualities other than a foreign name. It remains to be seen whether the great prestige of foreign firms, regardless of what they have to offer and the quality of it, is merely a passing fashion and the Chinese will come to trust the home product again in future. But before that, a Chinese practice like HPA will have to make its presence felt amidst fierce competition, fighting against foreign practices for a shrinking market.

We do this by offering a comprehensive service with the same contact person throughout the planning process, but also through increasing emphasis on non-standardized Chinese designs. The fact is that all too frequently a planning job in China is dealt with by simply copying earlier models or just building the same estate again on a different site. Years of experience make it possible for us to achieve an impressive result with financial and technical resources that are often extremely limited.

Integrating Western colleagues

But even that is not enough to hold our own against foreign competition. For this reason, the practice has employed some *waiguoren*

– "outside-country-people" – itself, and they have noticeably internationalized the practice culture. Close contact between Chinese and foreign colleagues means that interest in the "outside" has increased even more, and attempts are made to learn a great deal from each other.

The "long noses" considerably enhance HPA's prestige with the world about us. As soon as a foreigner presents a project to a client, confidence in the design increases.

Ill. 6.2: The so-called Cyber Tower stands near to the central People Square in downtown Shanghai.

As well as working as a design practice, HPA has established a second base as a local partner office for foreign practices. On the one hand, Chinese clients come to us to commission working plans for designs that have already been completed, but, on the other, there have been collaborations for many years, from an early planning phase onwards, with partner practices like DDG (Development Design Group) of Baltimore.

The practice and
procurement

The HPA architecture practice lives on follow-up contracts. As is customary in China, business contacts – *guanxi* – are very tightly de-

Ill. 6.3: A 35-storey office tower rises out of a five-storey base zone.

veloped and depend very strongly on personal sympathies. If a relationship of trust remains intact, clients will keep coming back and not start laboriously building up new building contacts. So HPA's first client, the owners of No. 2 Department Store, awarded the working planning for the second building phase of its most recent residential contract in spring 2005, as we had been responsible for designing the first phase.

Even when there are management changes in the finance and development firms, personal contacts remain. Someone looking to put up a building will usually turn to the architects he knew from his previous firm when he moves on. So the client base grows of its own accord, for as long as HPA does its work to the client's satisfaction.

Direct marketing is still handled, as is generally the custom in Europe, exclusively through distributing the company brochure and via the website.

We still take part in competitions if the commission is a particularly interesting one. For example, commissions for conspicuous high-rise buildings can only be acquired through competitions, unless an internationally known design practice is able to entice clients with its name and prestige. As competitions are not anonymous, but also strongly influenced by personal presentation, here again the image-gain brought about by the "in-house foreigner" is an advantage.

Entering competitions

Ill. 6.4: The masterplan covers 119 hectares and extends along a main road through the new Suzhou Industrial Park, in the form of two parallel, differently textured zones.

But competitions too are often decided by existing social contacts. Architects the client knows personally are invited to enter the competition, and winners can also be decided at a socio-political level. For example, in several competitions with exactly the same entrants, two different winners have been fixed quite deliberately, so that both of them will have a commission and no one will have to lose face.

Special aspects of client care

And that is exactly why it is so important to maintain personal contacts: whether by inviting people to dinner, including a lavish array of drinks or by meeting the craziest architectural requests – the customer is king. It frequently occurs that a client comes up to us with a concrete sketch or sample photographs and expects his ideas to be implemented precisely. On the other hand, developers are always careful to consider their own customers' ideas when selling them buildings, homes or shops. It is customary, for example, to plan a shopping centre without knowing exactly who will be owning or using it later. A glossy brochure and a large-scale model are produced, and the project marketing can begin. This often means that purchasers or tenants completely revise the plans, as the dimensions of the units do not meet their needs.

Many clients or their representatives have no specialist knowledge and make their decisions on a gut feeling. For this reason, HPA's planners always try to "educate" their clients a little when talking to them and take away their fear of the unknown. As most building projects are intended for sale, for financiers the ratio of experimental building and usable floor space to profit has to be maximized. Some psychological sensitivity is needed to persuade a client of the benefits of such crucial items as a central air-conditioning system rather than individual splintered units, or double rather than single glazing. A lot of materials and details often have to be cut down for financial reasons, but the building phase often also comes to grief because of lack of expertise in the firms involved.

Planning contracts

The contract side is much influenced by *guanxi* as well. Even though there is a written contract from the outset, everything is negotiable. In this respect, commercial life is very Asiatic.

The contract defines the commission and the scope of the work, the remuneration and the time frame. But if deadlines, which are always too tight, are not met, the client will content himself with an excuse. Conversely, it is very difficult to recover late payments legally, and imposing interest would be unthinkable.

Architects' remuneration is strongly determined by the market. Thus a foreign practice promoting itself in terms of exclusivity and without a local office will receive a higher fee than a local Chinese office for the same work on the basis of higher wages in the USA or in Europe. As local wages are so low, a different price for different bidders is entirely justified. But as soon as a branch with Chinese staff is opened, the prices usually fall. Nowadays a foreign name alone is not enough to justify a higher price. HPA with its quality and achievements is in the top third of Chinese offices, and in the bottom third internationally. Fees are usually set according to the area being worked on and the requisite building quality – furnishings, equipment and technical standards; they are not linked with building costs. As Chinese clients often say nothing about the actual building costs and these are difficult to determine anyway, it has become customary to tie the fee to area. This sum includes all the costs and expenses associated with the project, with the exception of printing costs for plans or presentations; travel expenses are included, and sometimes considerable extra work for repeated changes to the spatial programme. These have to be negotiated at the same time as the contract is concluded if they are to be paid in addition to the basic fee.

Remuneration for work

It is usual for payment to be made on completion of each phase of the work. Unfortunately, clients frequently insist that the work is not complete and retain the payment, or also that a project is broken down into various building stages after the contract is concluded and no payment is made until the last building stage. In situations like this, the practice has to finance the whole building phase in advance, which HPA has fortunately always been able to do.

Fee payments

Because wages for local workers are still low and office rents affordable, HPA architects are able to work very profitably.

The final expenditure on a project depends on how precisely the client knows what he wants. This is often not very precisely at all, so that fundamental changes have to be made throughout the course of the project and right up to the final stages. Normally we implement these changes without an additional fee in exchange for a relationship of trust between client and architect.

Usually between one and three people work on a particular project, and additional assistants are co-opted onto the team only at periods of high deadline pressure. As deadlines are regularly very tight, there is always enough for an individual worker on a project to do. So several project workers tend to work one after the other rather than working in parallel or staggered in phases: the project

Commercial viability of projects

stays with the same worker, but he or she can then turn to another project if there is a pause in the first.

Scope of work

The HPA practice offers three different service packages – with variants. Firstly, our Grade 1 Licence and the specialist engineers associated with it allows us to offer turnkey planning, from concept via design and working plans to construction and site supervision. We usually look after our local projects in Shanghai ourselves until completion. For projects in other Chinese provinces, we generally hand construction over to local planning practices because of different building laws but also because of the distances involved. In such cases HPA works as the design architect, who will draw up the preliminary and final design, is involved with the local authorities at the building permission stage, but otherwise supports working planning only in an advisory capacity. Conversely, HPA is responsible for working plans for other architects. These are usually foreign practices with no licence in China, but they can also be large Chinese practices who do not want to handle the working planning and site supervision themselves.

How the planning process runs

The office structures allow for specially designated colleagues who concentrate exclusively on working and construction plans and are very experienced at this; others are responsible for new designs. So the internal handover of a project from the design to the construction stage is similar to the handover of a project from another practice to HPA. Only the particular project manager is there from the beginning to the end.

The planning, permission and realization sequence functions largely like the American system with SD (Schematic Design), DD (Design Development), CD (Construction Design) and site supervision. Discussions with clients and the authorities are often informal and arranged at very short notice. Even so, perfect visual presentations and coloured sample images are expected at a very early stage, and these support the decision-making process. The whole project can stand or fall immediately if an individual decision-maker, the mayor, for example, likes or dislikes a rendering. We submit the approved plans with our architects' stamp as well as the presentation panels and a presentation book.

Depth and nature of planning presentation

Planning cannot always be conducted in such great detail as in the USA or Europe because of the constant rush. The emphasis is on a building's outward appearance, in particular. Function follows form, and experimental ground plans are not desirable as they are not as easy to market as the old familiar patterns of apartments, shops or offices that can be seen all over the country.

The details are seldom drawn on a large scale, but instead discussed in practical terms on site and in cooperation with the firms who will be responsible for them. Unduly complicated details would anyway not mean much, as Chinese building workers are not usually well educated and have no specialist training. For this reason, computer-generated perspectives are very important, as they can be referred to in case of doubt. A great deal hangs on these images, which are produced by outside rendering firms instructed by the design architect concerned.

Rendering firms break jobs down into particular specialities, so that three people work on each project as a rule. The first draws up the computer model on the basis of the architect's plans, who has to be constantly at his side to offer support and corrections. Next, colours and materials are allotted according to the architect's wishes. We have to pay particular attention at this stage to prevent the computer experts, most of whom have no design training, from making incorrect decisions. After the viewing angle and focal depth of the "photograph" have been agreed, the image is rendered and given a final polish by the addition of people, cars, trees, etc. The individual stages have to be checked and adjusted constantly to ensure that the end product will look as the architect wishes.

The large amount of time spent on computer perspectives is justified by the importance accorded to them. The fate of a project is decided by the quality of the renderings, from the first presentations to the client onwards. They are in large formats on high-gloss paper, and can show even the lay public what the project will look like in reality. The computer perspectives are used as direct models in the building phase, as mentioned above.

Very rapidly progressing projects and the culture of the "self-made man" in China often lead to chaotic organization. Many processes are constantly being reinvented, so that it is impossible to establish a standard and those involved have to find their bearings again each time. This affects all planning areas and project execution, both inside the office and in terms of contact with clients. For example, it is not unusual for business e-mails to be read only when the recipient is notified about the arrival of the e-mail on the phone. It is also quite common for an entire company to have a joint electronic mailbox. Some time can pass before the appropriate information reaches the recipient.

Both internal and external communication depends very much on individuals, as information is not usually recorded in writing. As

Special project
realization features

HPA's employees usually stay with the firm for a long time, knowledge can be passed on to colleagues. But for many companies in China staff turnover is very high, so that the premises can change fundamentally with each new contact. This can mean that even planning that is nearing completion can collapse, or at least many matters that have already been resolved may have to be discussed again.

Cooperation and branches

As well as its main branch in Shanghai, HPA has had a branch in Beijing since 2001. At first this specialized exclusively in interior design, but at present the architecture side is growing strongly. The Beijing office is looked after by Haiqing Wu from Shanghai, but does some of its own procurement locally.

Ill. 6.5: The Shanghai electricity company's new headquarters was created by converting a half-finished, insolvent building ruin.

Ill. 6.6: Electric Tower, passage

Both HPA offices regularly work with other practices, usually foreign ones, on particular projects, as has already been mentioned.
Contacts are often established on a personal basis, before cooperation can be considered. The precise team hierarchy in the office is
being constantly redefined: sometimes people work together on an
equal footing, sometimes a job is split or two parallel alternatives
devised, and sometimes HPA is the on-site contact architect, helping
the designing practice with its administration.

Years of work together tie us to the American practice DDG (Development Design Group), with whom we have completed some commercial projects, but also some luxury residential projects. We won the competition for the new German School in Shanghai with the German architecture practice Bauwerk of Münster, though another local office took over the final planning stage.

We also work with landscape architects from elsewhere. Many of our buildings are linked with outdoor planning by the ADI's Hongkong landscape architects, and we also have links with firms in Singapore and even Europe.

When working with someone else in the design phase, the partner architect will usually survey the planning site with us, perhaps remain on the spot for a first workshop and then develop the more precise planning details in his home country. Communication is then by e-mail and telephone with HPA's English-speaking colleagues. If problems arise with Chinese contacts we sometimes work as direct interpreters and mediators in a telephone conference. In this way linguistic and intercultural misunderstandings can be cleared up in conversation. The two architecture practices appear together at client presentations and visits to local authorities.

If HPA is functioning as a local architect for a different designer, we try to understand the designer's ideas as well as possible, so that they can be implemented as precisely as possible. Constant contact between HPA and the design architect during the final planning and construction stages means that corrections can be made where needed. As a practice with a great deal of experience in China we are in a position to achieve the desired result, despite compromises relating to the budget or choice of materials, through careful detailed planning and sometimes protracted conversations with the firms who are carrying out the work.

Legal questions and legal certainty

Although the Chinese legal system has now grown to a considerable extent, many questions are still resolved at an informal level. The Chinese themselves rely on their good relationships with each other and regulate their lives together through mutual give and take. Foreigners are usually expected to give more than they take, however.

HPA's partners, Paul Chen and Haiqing Wu, accumulated extensive experience of the American legal system in their ten years in the USA, so the differences are particularly clear here. Since setting up the joint company in Shanghai, we have usually resolved disputes with clients and subcontractors in conversation. Lawyers are seldom called in, and even then little happens other than threatening proceedings.

The Chinese legal system is increasingly shifting towards protecting the weaker party. This increases the chances of pushing home justifiable demands for fees in cases of dispute. As the other party is also aware of this, threats of proceedings are taken seriously and usually lead to the sum due being paid.

Architects' mistakes can often be dealt with by a sincerely meant apology. A tolerant attitude to the client's requests will be requested in return. Sometimes considerable extra time and effort spent on new variants and changes is the price for a carefree life as far as the architect's liability is concerned.

Another problem is that work is sometimes published without permission being sought, which infringes copyright law. As intellectual property is not anchored in everyday Chinese culture, proceedings instigated by an individual would simply be like water off a duck's back. As so many images are published, buildings are becoming increasingly better known and, since this is partly in the architect's own interest, nothing is usually done about such small infringements.

Copyright problems

As Chinese law does not insist on personal insurance for architects, the HPA practice is only minimally insured. It is usual for the client to take on insurance costs for the project phase, and thus meet expenses for damages arising from errors.

Insuring the practice

The standard government-recommended contract, which we use with minor variations, provides for maximum liability for architects to the level of the full project fee. This means that in the worst case we could have worked for nothing. In the case of major damage caused by a very high degree of negligence, a court can impose withdrawal of the licence as the maximum punishment. This means that a practice can no longer work independently, which is why this extreme case should be avoided to the best of one's ability.

However, if the *gaunxi* relations are intact, and both sides visibly do their best, it will not come to that, and even major errors are forgiven as human.

Prospects for the future

After almost a decade and a half of architectural work we intend in future to strive to create an international atmosphere in the office and in our customer contacts. We will carry out an increasing number of projects outside China in order to enhance the extent to which we are known outside the region. Partnerships with international ar-

Ill. 6.7: Royal Garden is a luxurious residential quarter on the southern outskirts of Shanghai offering a great deal of open space and park-style living in the most confined space possible.

Ill. 6.8: Low-, mid- and high-rise residential blocks stand in a staggered arrangement around the central garden axis on a linear basis.

chitecture practices are to be further extended and strengthened. The commissions we accept will move more in the direction of public and commercial projects and away from standardized housing construction, but the number of employees is not to be increased, as too few colleagues would know each other as office numbers grew to guarantee appropriate communication.

As a private planning office in Shanghai, we constantly strive for high design quality combined with the best possible service. HPA's architects have proved this with numerous projects over a considerable range of activities, including master planning, office buildings, commercial and housing projects, educational and leisure facilities and interior design. This portfolio has gained HPA high standing in specialist and client circles, and numerous buildings have been honoured with specialist prizes and publications.

About the author:
Kerstin Hartmann studied architecture from 1993 to 2000 at the Technische Universität in Munich and from 1995 to 1996 at the Technische Universität in Graz.
After working as an Assistant Architect for JMP John McAslan + Partner in London from 2000 to 2001, doing freelance work for ITGA in Gauting in 2002, and working as an architect and project manager for PA GmbH Papadopoulos Associates in Munich from 2002 to 2003, Kerstin Hartmann has been Associate Architect with HPA HaiPo Architects in Shanghai since late 2003.

Appendix

E 1   Contact addresses

Authors

Dr. Bert Bielefeld / Lars-Phillip Rusch
www.bauwesen.uni-dortmund.de

Dr. Andreas Szesny
www.qgsc.com

Matthias Wehrlin
www.wehrlin.ch

Dr. Christian Gloyer
www.bgkw-law.de

Hans-Peter Holler
www.dreso.com/china

Werner Sübai
www.hpp.com

Scott Romses
www.romsesarchitects.com

Stephan Jentsch
www.pjar.com

Bruno Braun
www.brunobraun-architekten.de

Kerstin Hartmann
www.hpa.cn

Nikolaus Goetze
www.gmp-architekten.de

Gordon Brandenfels
www.brandenfels.com

Quinn Lu / Michael Pruss
www.werkhart.com

Embassies and Consulates

German Embassy in China

German Embassy in the People's Republic of China
17, Dongzhimenwai Dajie, Chaoyang
Beijing 100600
PR China
Tel.: 0086 / 10 / 65 32 21 61
Fax: 0086 / 10 / 65 32 53 36
E-Mail: embassy@peki.diplo.de

Chinese Embassy in Germany

Embassy of the People's Republic of China
Märkisches Ufer 54
10179 Berlin
Tel.: 0049 / 30 / 27 58 8 0
Fax: 0049 / 30 / 27 58 8 221
E-Mail: chinaemb_de@mfa.gov.cn
www.china-botschaft.de

Consular Department of the Embassy of the People's Republic of China
Brückenstrasse 10
10179 Berlin
Tel.: 0049 / 30 / 27 588 572
Fax: 0049 / 30 / 27 588 519

British Embassy in China

British Embassy Consular Section
Kerry Centre 1, Guanghualu,
Beijing, 100020
Tel.: 00 86 / 10 / 85 29 66 00
Fax: 00 86 / 10 / 85 29 60 81
E-Mail: consularmailbeijing@fco.gov.uk

Chinese Embassy in the UK

Embassy of the People's Republic of China
49 Portland Place
London
W1B 1QL
Tel.: 0044 / 20 / 7299 4049

US Embassy in China

United States Embassy of Beijing
Ambassador Clark T. Randt, Jr.
Xiu Shue Bei Jie 3, 100600
Tel.: 00 86 / 10 / 65 32 38 31
Fax: 00 86 / 10 / 65 32 20 39

Chinese Embassy in the USA

Embassy of the People's Republic of China
2201 Wisconsin Avenue, N.W.
Washington D.C. 20007
Tel.: 00 1 / 202 / 338 6688
Fax: 00 1 / 202 / 588 9760

French Embassy in China

Ambassade de France en Chine
3, San Li Tun Dongsanjie, Chaoyang District,
Pékin 100600
Tel.: 00 86 / 10 / 85 32 80 80
Fax: 00 86 / 10 / 85 32 48 41
Internet: www.ambafrance-cn.org

Chinese Embassy in France

Ambassade de la République Populaire de Chine en France
9, Avenue Victor Cresson
92130 Issy Les Moulineaux
Tel.: 0033 / 1 / 01 47 36 00 71
Fax: 0033 / 1 / 47 36 34 46
Internet: www.amb-chine.fr

Austrian Embassy in China

Österreichische Botschaft Peking
Jianguomenwai, Xiushui Nanjie 5,
100600 Peking
Tel.: 00 86 / 10 / 65 32 20 61
Fax: 00 86 / 10 / 65 32 15 05
E-Mail: peking-ob@bmaa.gv.at

Chinese Embassy in Austria

Internet: www.chinaembassy.at

Chinese Embassy in Switzerland

Botschaft der Volksrepublik China
Kalcheggweg 10,
3006 Bern
Tel.: 0041 / 31 / 352 73 33
Fax: 0041 / 31 / 352 73 34
Internet: www.china-embassy.ch

Section consulaire Visa
Tel.: 0041 / 31 / 351 45 93

Other Internet addresses:

German Foreign Office
www.auswaertiges-amt.de

Net architecture export by the Bundesarchitektenkammer (Federal Chamber of Architects)
www.architekturexport.de

Contact platform for German planners
www.planned-in-germany.de

Bundesagentur für Aussenwirtschaft (German Foreign Trade Agency)
www.bfai.de

Deutsche Aussenhandelskammer China (Chamber of Foreign Trade for China)
www.china.ahk.de

IHK Köln (main Chamber for China)
http://www.ihk-koeln.de

Sinolog Projektservice Ostasien GmbH (Eastern Asian Project Service)
www.sinolog.de

Royal Institute of British Architects
www.riba.org

Architectes Français à l' Export
www.archi.fr/afex

Col.legi d'Arquitectes de Catalunya
www.coac.net/international

E 2   Bibliography

Chapter A 2

- Bauer, Wolfgang: *China und die Hoffnung auf Glück*. Deutscher Taschenbuch Verlag: Munich, 1990.
- *China Daily*: *"Forum hears voices for sustainable development"*. Beijing, 7. 10. 2005, p. 5.
- Chung, Judy; Inaba, Jeffrey; Koolhaas, Rem; Leong, Sze Tsung (eds.): *Project on the City 1: Great Leap Forward*. Taschen: Cologne, 2001.
- Liang, Sicheng: *Zhongguo jianzhushi* (History of Chinese Architecture). Baihua wenyi chubanshe. Tianjin, 1998.
- Lü Junhua, Peter G. Rowe, Zhang Jie (eds.): *Modern Urban Housing in CHINA 1840–2000*. Prestel: Munich, London, New York, 2001.
- Maar, Christa; Burda, Hubert (eds.): *Iconic Turn: Die neue Macht der Bilder*. DuMont: Cologne, 2004.
- Warner, Torsten: *Deutsche Architektur in China: Architekturtransfer*. Ernst & Sohn: Berlin, 1994.

Chapter A 3

- Albert Lutz, Museum Rietberg Zürich (ed.), *Dian. Ein versunkenes Königreich in China*; Verlag Museum Rietberg 1986.
- Liu Xue (ed.), *Spring City Kunming, The Past, the Present and the Future*; City of Kunming Press 2004.
- Chenggong of Kunming, P.R. China; The Regulatory Plan of Chenggong, 2005 planning report, can be downloaded as a pdf at www.wehrlin/publikationen.
- Carl Fingerhuth, Ernst Joost (ed.), *The Kunming Project. Urban Development in China – a Dialogue*; Birkhäuser Verlag: Basel Boston Berlin, 2002.

E 3   Index